WINNING WITH SOCIAL SELLING

WINNING WITH SOCIAL SELLING

*Strategies and Techniques to Build Your Brand,
Network, and Net Worth*

Mark Ghaderi

PARTRIDGE

A Penguin Random House Company

ISBN:	Hardcover	978-1-4828-6928-6
	Softcover	978-1-4828-6927-9
	eBook	978-1-4828-6926-2

To order additional copies of this book, contact
Partridge India
000 800 10062 62
orders.india@partridgepublishing.com

www.partridgepublishing.com/india

This book is a must read for anyone who wants to be a successful salesperson in the age of social media. It's packed with relevant information and actionable tips that will boost your sales and put more money in your pockets.

Kevin Mizuhara
Marketing and sales consultant
Entrepreneur
Redwood Shores, California

As a Sales Executive who up until now has used more traditional sales methods, I found the book to be extremely informative and helpful in understanding the foundation of social selling and I strongly recommend it to any Sales Professional for both B2B and B2C sales activities. This book will help you to get there fast and avoid all the mistakes you would make if you go at it alone.

Farzam Hadi
President of Oriens K.K.
Sales leader & executive
Tokyo

COMMUNITY MATTERS

As a member of my community I look forward to any opportunity to give back to my community in some small way. One of the charity organizations that I often support is the Special Olympics. As the Special Olympics organization puts it "This is a global movement that touches and changes lives for persons with intellectual disabilities through the transformative power of sports."

Publishing this book gives me a great pleasure as I want to share my success with one of my favorite charities. I will be donating 30% of the proceeds from the sales of my book "Winning With Social Selling" to the Special Olympics of Singapore.

Rest assured that you not only personally benefit by buying (and reading) this book, you also help to support a worthy cause that brings joy to an aspiring athlete and everyone around this remarkable and special member of our global community.

Mark Ghaderi

DEDICATION

TO MY DAUGHTER AND SON, ELENOR AND MAXWELL WHO HAVE GIVEN MEANING TO MY LIFE AND MADE ME FEEL JOYS AND PAINS MORE INTENSE THAN I EVER THOUGHT POSSIBLE. I HAVE LOVED YOU BOTH BEFORE YOU CAME INTO MY LIFE, AND WILL LOVE YOU AND BE PROUD OF YOU UNTIL I LEAVE YOURS.

Acknowledgement

I would like to express my heartfelt appreciation and gratitude to a lot of people who have supported me in writing this book. Firstly I like to thank my family for giving me their support and encouraging me to keep going, even though it took away from our family time at nights and weekends. I also want to thank my friends and colleagues who helped me shape and structure my thoughts and ideas around a very big topic, offered me on-going feedback and cheered me on.

I most certainly want to express my gratitude to the business leaders and sales professionals who have honored me by attending my sessions, sharing their stories, giving me feedback and allowing me the opportunity to learn from them.

A big THANKS to my manager and mentor, Chema who encouraged me to take the plunge and start writing about this and other topics that I am passionate about.

I especially like to thank the LinkedIn team, especially Shweta, Krishna and of course Koka for their generous support and being my biggest enablers.

The team at We Are Social have been absolutely fantastic in generously sharing their mountain of data on social media and allowing me to share them with you. In addition I want to thank Kathy Hadley for allowing me to share her blog content on the benefits of Facebook Fan Page.

Finally a great big THANKS goes to the kind and hardworking crew at the Northpoint and Woodlands Civic center Starbucks stores who kept me awake and focused. You guys are awesome!

Foreword

Social selling has been whispered about or openly discussed in the board room for the past few years. Ever since the invention of the telephone technology has been accelerating the sales process. Email changed the game again allowing sales professionals to scale communications across multiple buyers. Recently there has been a monumental shift in the buying process that has made the phone and email a sales method become less effective.

It takes on average 8 attempts to get contact with a decision maker. Multiply that out across all of the accounts your sales teams are working on, time is not in your favor if you rely on the traditional methods of smile and dial. Just as buyers have evolved to leverage social media in the buying process, sales professionals have to get more involved and even strive to become experts in the use of social media as a sales tool. Social selling is the method for finding and engaging buyers on social networks where trust and information drives business.

You need to adapt or you risk being left behind. Training your sales teams to look for sales triggers on social media and best practices on how to connect with these decision makers will build your pipeline. The task of moving from online to offline is one of the most important skills a social selling professional can learn to be successful in this decade.

Building your online profiles to be a resource to your buyers becomes one of the largest assets you have as a sales professional. Leveraging that professional brand to fill your pipeline with social buyers builds on itself over time to make you a primary resource for your industry.

Relationships turn into revenue when your strategy is to provide value in excess of your cost. Your social selling methodology should be comprehensive and should push you out of your comfort zone to develop new skills that are more like an investment in your professional career.

I have been helping companies with social selling since before it had a name. I met Mark on my travels through APAC and I was impressed with his knowledge on the subject and his eagerness to find better ways to train sales professionals on how to use social media. When Mark reached out to me about this book, I was happy to read through it and give my thoughts. What I got out of this book was more than I expected.

This book covers so many aspects of social selling that it can be valuable to a sales professional through their entire career. The research to how businesses in Asia Pacific countries shows a clear reason to get involved with social selling now and the impact it can have.

Being social means nothing if you don't know what networks to be active on. Mark covers how to identify the right networks and then drills into how to leverage these networks to drive the largest business impact. This book will help you hit your number.

Koka Sexton - Forbes #1 Social Selling Expert

Founder Social Selling Labs

A note on sources:

Since many of the sources I have used are online and I want to minimize the number of printed pages the bibliography and information on sources of data used have been placed online and are available by going to the following link:

www.winningwithsocialselling.com/booksources

Contents

"Internalize the Golden Rule of sales that says: All things being equal, people will do business with, and refer business to, those people they know, like and trust."

– Bob Burg

"Eagles don't flock."

– Ross Perot

Introduction

First, I want to congratulate you on taking this crucial step to educate yourself further, and enhance your potential for personal & financial success through better understanding and use of the social media. If you are reading this book, it means you already have realized the ever-growing importance and relevance of social media in better serving your clients and becoming more successful as a company or a sales professional.

If you have been in sales or any customer facing role, you already know that the job of selling and serving your clients has become a lot more complicated. The job of finding and effectively engaging new clients has also become a more challenging task. There are many reasons for this, including the fact that there is too much noise, too many distractions and too many ever-shifting preferences and priorities in everyone's life and business.

Yet, in some ways, the job of selling has become easier than ever before, partly thanks to technological innovations and the global reach of the internet and social media. These new tools (many of which are less than ten years old), allows us to communicate with a single person or millions of people across the globe in seconds! The social media is truly a powerful tool that as sales professionals, we all need to understand, learn and embrace if we want to remain relevant and be successful.

Before we start, I want to make a promise that after you finish reading this book and start using the presented techniques, ideas and tools on daily basis consistently, you will see positive sales and pipeline results within few weeks or months depending on your industry and business.

I also want to encourage you to visit the 'Resources' section of our website www.winningwithsocialselling.com where you will have access to a host of up-to-date resources, content, tools, templates and tips on how to maximize your return on social selling efforts.

The intended readers of this book are the following: sales executives & managers, business owners, marketing managers, telemarketing & demand generation specialists who carry revenue or pipeline generation targets, along with anyone else who wants to have a successful business.

Regardless of being a millennial generation sales professional with 20,000 followers or an old timer with 20 years of experience in complex, multimillion-dollar sales, you will benefit from reading this book.

In this book, I will discuss how to systematically decide the right social channels for your business, and how to build a 'social brand' that will get you connected with the right target audience, FAST! I will also share with you recent statistics on various social media platforms and their market size.

For those of you who live and work in the Asia Pacific region, or have business in the region, you will find the chapter "Getting Social in Asia Pacific" a great resource as I will share with you the social media usage in the region's major markets and discuss general cultural context of social media in the region. I have lived and worked in the Asia Pacific region for over 17 years. During this time I have consulted, advised, trained or sold to hundreds of companies, and have been involved in three start-ups. I will provide you with practical guides and tips on how to use social media in Asia's key markets.

You will find the latest crucial statistics on key global and local social platforms and where you should spend your money and time to maximize your return in these markets. I will be discussing in detail what you need to do to establish yourself as an approachable GO-TO expert and thought leader in your field of expertise.

What I am talking about here is your "BRAND" and how to build a brand that helps you be more successful in your business.

But before we get into the tactical do's and don'ts of social selling, it is important to have an effective strategy that will help you guide your activities and meet your goals. In chapters three and four I will discuss the steps you should take to plan and execute an effective social selling strategy.

With that said, let's start to build you the RIGHT network because going forward **your network = your net worth.**

"It's not the strongest of the species that survive,
But the ones that are responsive to change"

– Charles Darwin

Chapter 1

The New Buying Trends

Change is….everywhere

In my 20+ years in business & sales leadership, I have come to depend on one thing in business that remains constant: CHANGE. But as they say, 'CHANGE IS GOOD!'. Change is what creates the need to buy.

At the same time, change is often our biggest challenge in selling. Think about the Global Financial Crisis of 2008. What did that massive and unpleasant economic change do for businesses around the world? If you were in any quota carrying role at that point, what happened to your sales pipeline overnight? It sure wasn't pleasant for me to see my pipeline evaporate within days.

You may say, 'change is part of life'; and you would be right. However, what is different now is the ever accelerating speed of change that has made our jobs as sales professionals so much harder. In large part, this has been due to advancements in science and technology that are changing the world around us at an unprecedented speed. To be successful in selling in such a dynamic environment requires a great deal of agility and focus.

Power shift

There has been a great power shift in favor of the consumers against the product manufacturers and service providers. Today's customers are much less likely to wait for a vendor to get back to them or show a great deal of loyalty to a particular vendor if they don't feel that they are getting good service. Not long ago, the vendor enjoyed a stronger bargaining position and had the power to dictate how to interact with its customers.

The main reason for this shift in power is information. As they say, 'knowledge is power'. This is certainly true when it comes to making a purchase. Today, we all have access to virtually unlimited amount of information on any topic by just going online. Customers no longer have to depend on vendors to learn about and evaluate products and services. Today's buyers often times are more knowledgeable than the sales executives they are buying from. If you want to buy or learn about anything such as a car, house, medical care, education, travel…etc., your first stop will be the internet, right? Within minutes you will have all the information you need to make a better buying decision.

Reluctance to engage

Having an ocean of information ready to flow out of your computer, Tablet or your cell phone has led to another trend in the world: The ability for the buyer to avoid engaging a sales person as long as possible, and if feasible avoid it all together. Reluctance to engage with the sales person is nothing new. Let's face it, Nobody likes to talk to sales people unless they have to. Even sales people don't want to talk to a sales person. A survey by Forester in 2011 revealed that the buying cycle is almost 70% complete before the buyer engages the sales person.

This is a seismic shift from the traditional buying process. Today's customers no longer need to talk to a vendor to learn about the solutions, specifications and availability. They often go online and do the initial rounds of research, fact gathering, internal discussions and vendor elimination before contacting a selected number of vendors to finalize the purchase.

This buying model leaves less room for the sales executive to do a lot of initial discovery, analysis and rapport building. With the current model, the sales person who comes into the conversation two-third of the way into the buying cycle would have a lot less opportunity to shape the client's opinion on what they should do.

What this means is that if you want to be in the top 20% of sales executives who get to meet and overachieve their revenue targets through stronger customer relationship, you must get actively engaged with your prospects before they recognize the need for your products and services.

So, what to do? How to get in front of the potential clients before they are ready to hear from you? The answer to this question of course is to USE

SOCIAL MEDIA! A study done by IDC has shown that majority of B2B buyers are using the social media platforms to gather information and learn about their buying options. It is clear that the social media has become part of our lives and has reached a tipping point on becoming a viable business communication tool that if used properly, could change and shape opinions and strategies.

Global Village

For thousands of years, humans lived in small communities and relied on personal relationships with others in the community to get through life challenges. Today, not much has changed, except that the villages have become much bigger in population and the technology has made the world a much smaller place where billions of people are sharing the planet, experiences, photos, videos and emoticons. Not surprising, we are still depending on each other to help make choices in life, including buying decisions. Today, as the internet has become available in every corner of the planet, the network, and more specifically the **social network**, has become a way for buyers to research and get feedback from others about what products and services they should buy.

Insight, not information

We are all looking for insight and not just information. These days we are all familiar with the concept of giving favorite or not so favorite opinion/stars/thumbs up or down to a restaurant, movie, product or service online. This is how we are telling others how we feel and think about a particular vendor or service. We are taking pictures of our food at restaurants and clothes we buy, or want to buy, and posting them online for everyone to see and comment on. We often add our comments as well and expect others to do the same. These are all personal insights that we are sharing with the world online and almost instantly through images words and sounds.

Importance of value justification

We, as with any living organism, are programmed at our DNA level to look out for our own best interests. This has not changed much over time. As personal or business consumers we are seeking the same. However, In recent years, thanks to technological advances, it has become easier for us to shop around and evaluate on our own where we could get the best perceived value.

But in recent years the level of uncertainty and perceived risk in business, brought home by events such as the Global Financial Crisis of 2008, and the European financial crises has made the need to show faster & more tangible business values in business to business purchases a MUST. This need for seeking greater value in a shorter timeline has made it necessary for the sales organizations to re-think the traditional approach to selling through functions, features & technical specs. Instead, the sales organizations need to focus on business justifications that align with each buyer's unique needs and desires. This need for identifying relevant business justifications for each target client has made it necessary for the sales executives to learn more about the prospect and his/her priorities before even engaging with them. A recent IDC survey has Shown that today's clients don't engage with the vendors until most of the buying process is completed. Therefore the sales executives can no longer wait for the prospect to contact them, because by then it may be too late and the sales opportunity is lost. We, as sales professionals, need to seek actionable insight about the prospect before we even approach our prospects. So, where do you think we find this kind of crucial insight?

"You are what you share."

– Charles W. Leadbeater

Chapter 2

What is Social Selling

Before we talk about HOW, let's talk a little bit about WHAT social selling is.

Social selling is a pretty new concept, born from the explosive growth and success of the social media networks that did not exist even a decade ago, with some claiming to have hundreds of millions, even billions of users. Social media could be defined as:

"exchanging ideas, information & insight through the internet and networks"

When you have such a dynamic and ever expanding network of billions of people sharing thoughts and ideas it is natural for businesses, governments, politicians, celebrities and everyone else to try to use it to influence others on what they think, wear, do, and buy. In other words, it is about using the social channels to sell.

Where is social media today?

Let's take a step back to look at the big picture and understand the market size and maturity of social media as a whole. Here are some statistics about the potential market size and the number of users across the globe from the survey done by We Are Social:

GLOBAL DIGITAL SNAPSHOT

A SNAPSHOT OF THE WORLS'S KEY DIGITAL STATISTICAL INDICATORS

TOTAL POPULATION	ACTIVE INTERNET USERS	ACTIVE SOCIAL MEDIA USERS	UNIQUE MOBILE USERS	ACTIVE MOBILE SOCIAL USERS

7,219 BILLION	**3,038 BILLION**	**2,126 BILLION**	**3,679 BILLION**	**1,753 BILLION**
URBANISATION: 53%	PENETRATION: 42%	PENETRATION: 29%	PENETRATION: 51%	PENETRATION: 24%
FIGURE REPRESENTATION TOTAL REIGONAL POPULATION, INCLUDING CHILDREN	FIGURE INCLUDES ACCESS VIA FIXED AND MOBILE CONNECTIONS	FIGURE REPRESENTS ACTIVE USER ACCOUNTS ON THE MOST ACTIVE SOCIAL PLATFORM,IN EACH COUNTRY,NOT UNIQUE USERS	FIGURE REPRESENTS MOBILE SUBSCRIPTIONS, NOT UNQUE USERS	FIGURE REPRESENTS ACTIVE USER ACCOUNTS ON THE MOST ACTIVE SOCIAL PLATFORM,IN EACH COUNTRY,NOT UNIQUE USER

We are social

MAR 2015

7

DAILY INTERNET ACTIVITY

BASED ON AVERAGE DAILY GLOBAL ACTIVITY

Image 2-02

| NUMBER OF GOOGLE SEARCHES CONDUCTED EACH DAY | NUMBER OF VIDEOS WATCHED ON EACH DAY | NUMBER OF SKYPE CALLS MADE EACH DAY |

205 BILLION   3.5 BILLION   8.4 BILLION   145 MILLION

We are social

MAR 2015

8

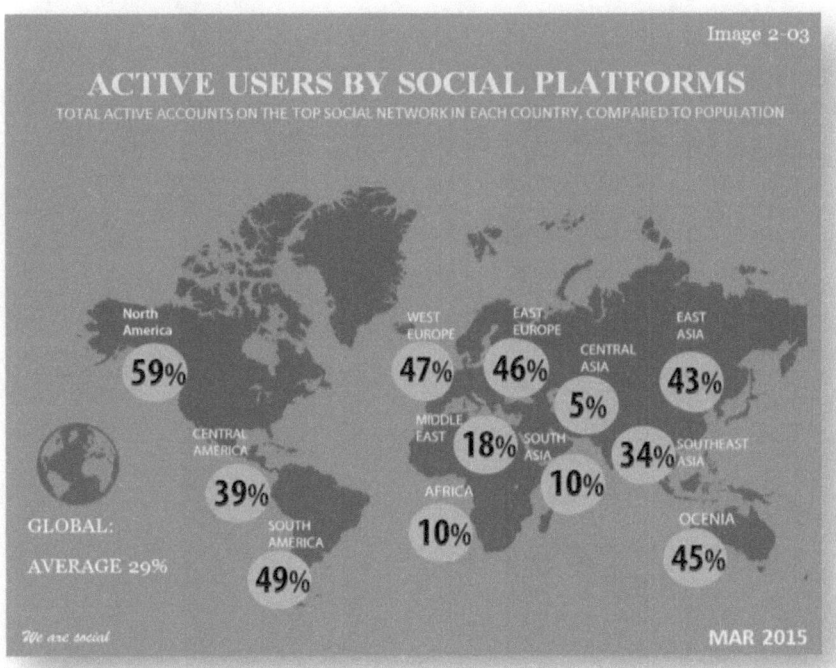

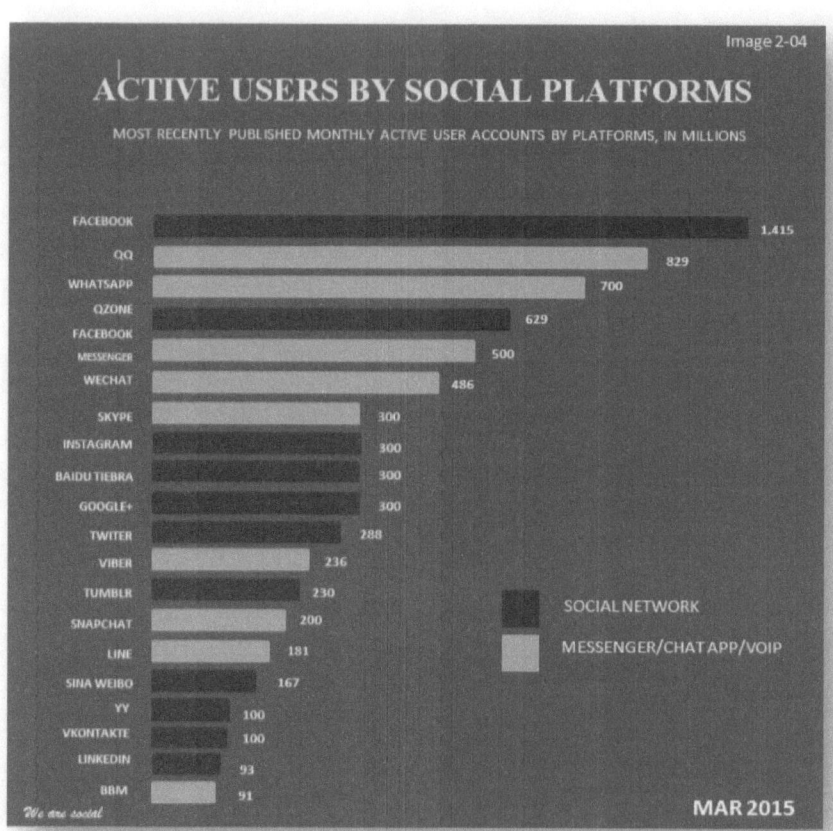

An interesting trend in recent years has been the increase in the use of mobile to access the internet and social media. There is already more cell phones that Personal Computers in the world. Using the cell phone to access the social channels is growing in double digits and will continue to do so with millions of new Smartphone users coming online and skipping the need for a desktop to get connected.

The trend to access social media through mobile devices is particularly strong among the younger users and also in many parts of the emerging markets in Asia and Africa. As you will see later for majority of the social media users around the world the cell phones are the primary method of accessing the social media channels.

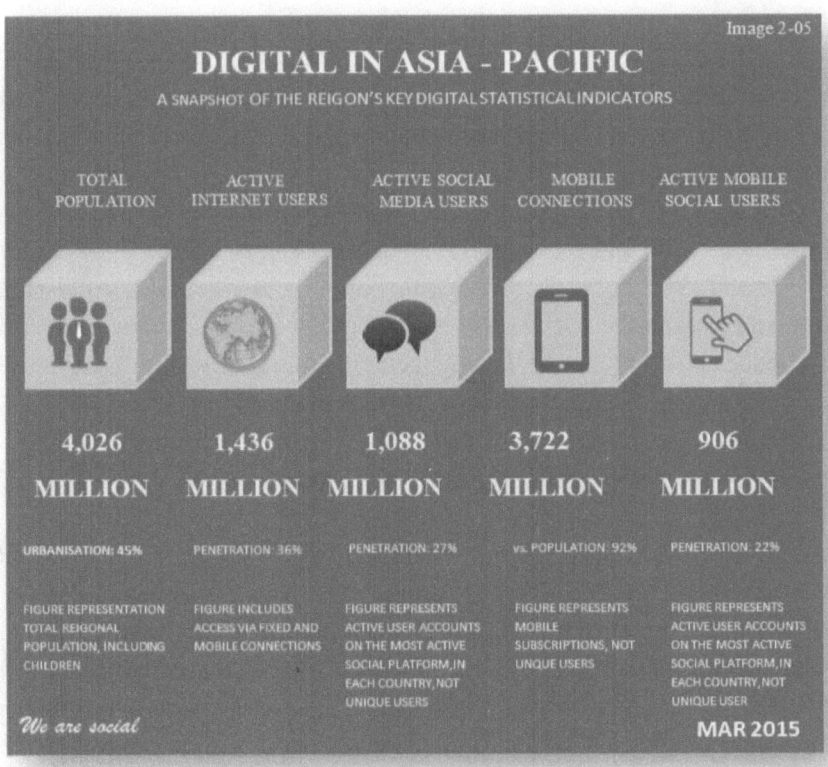

Image 2-05

DIGITAL IN ASIA - PACIFIC

A SNAPSHOT OF THE REIGON'S KEY DIGITAL STATISTICAL INDICATORS

TOTAL POPULATION	ACTIVE INTERNET USERS	ACTIVE SOCIAL MEDIA USERS	MOBILE CONNECTIONS	ACTIVE MOBILE SOCIAL USERS
4,026 MILLION	1,436 MILLION	1,088 MILLION	3,722 MILLION	906 MILLION
URBANISATION: 45%	PENETRATION: 36%	PENETRATION: 27%	vs. POPULATION: 92%	PENETRATION: 22%
FIGURE REPRESENTATION TOTAL REIGONAL POPULATION, INCLUDING CHILDREN	FIGURE INCLUDES ACCESS VIA FIXED AND MOBILE CONNECTIONS	FIGURE REPRESENTS ACTIVE USER ACCOUNTS ON THE MOST ACTIVE SOCIAL PLATFORM, IN EACH COUNTRY, NOT UNIQUE USERS	FIGURE REPRESENTS MOBILE SUBSCRIPTIONS, NOT UNQUE USERS	FIGURE REPRESENTS ACTIVE USER ACCOUNTS ON THE MOST ACTIVE SOCIAL PLATFORM, IN EACH COUNTRY, NOT UNIQUE USER

We are social

MAR 2015

Chapter 3

Leveraging Social Media in Selling

After looking at the social media user numbers and the size of the network you cannot help asking yourself the question "how can I turn these numbers into business opportunities?". Of course this is why you are reading this book!

Once you read and internalize the above stats you come to realize that using social media to build and serve your clients is no longer a 'nice to have'; it's a 'MUST HAVE' As a business owner, sales organization or sales professional you need to leverage the social channels to build a stronger engagement with your audience and turn your social engagements into revenue opportunities by adding value and differentiating yourself from the 'herd'.

The "selling" in social selling is still selling

As the old saying goes "THE MORE THINGS CHANGE, THE MORE THEY STAY THE SAME!". This is certainly true when it comes to the act of selling. One thing you must keep in mind that just because you have 10 different social channels available to you, that does not mean you no longer have to sell. After all, what is selling? Selling is about influencing other people's decisions on what to buy and where to buy it. Connecting with people or posting articles and pictures does not translate into selling until you take deliberate steps to engage and influence the buyer. The social media is just an amazingly more effective, scalable and personal way for you to reach the right people and influence their buying behaviors.

The social media has some key advantages that make it a great customer engagement tool. Here are some of the reasons why social media can help you to be more successful at what you are already doing:

Level the playing field

One of the major benefits of the internet and social networks is that they can work as equalizers, allowing for much smaller players to effectively compete and win against much bigger and better funded competitors. In today's fast moving world the fast and agile eats the slow and rigid. Every day I see companies and individuals who are changing the game by listening to their target audience and reaching them in new and creative ways through the social media channels and building their credibility and brand.

Be the first

Studies have shown that you have 50% better chance of winning the deal if you are the first sales person to reach the prospect. As the old saying goes "the early bird catches the worm". As we discussed earlier since customers are not engaging sellers until way into their buying cycle, you have to put yourself in the mind of your target customers way before they are thinking of your products and services. This is about branding yourself and owning a few cells in your prospect's brain so that when he/she needs the kind of solutions you offer, he/she thinks of you first without a lot of research and googling.

Let me illustrate what I mean by 'owning a few brain cells in your prospect's mind'. If I ask you to think of a luxury car, which brand name comes to your mind without much thinking? Rolls Royce, Mercedes? BMW...? Regardless of which brand you think of, that brand now owns a cell or two in your brain that drives to look for that brand of car if you are buying a luxury car, without even thinking about it. This is a powerful advantage over the competitors. With social media you could build your brand in the mind of your target client so that when they are ready to contact a vendor for your services, their brain will drive them to you.

Almost Real-time response

With social media you don't have to wait for days or weeks to capture and measure effectiveness of your efforts. If you have done your homework you will often know within minutes or hours if you are connecting with the right people. I have seen companies get ten times the response they would get from a 3 months long print campaign within one week from a well-orchestrated social media effort. The key is to understand the medium and have the right content in the right context.

I have seen thousands of blogs, twitters, LinkedIn profiles and facebook pages by business and I am here to tell you that over 90% of them have not figured it out yet. They either have the wrong media, wrong message or wrong everything. In this kind of environment it is easier for you to stand out and get noticed when you read, internalize and apply what you learn from my book. Remember in today's fast moving world if you want to get better at anything keep this as your motto: FAIL OFTEN AND FAST.

New approach to an old problem

Numerous surveys have shown some alarming findings about the way today's customers want to engage with vendors. Here are a few:

Less face time: It may be just my observation but I have noticed that today's buyers, particularly the younger generation are less likely to accept requests for face to face meetings and invitations for shows and seminars; specially early in the sales cycle. They are more comfortable with digital communication.

No cold calls: over 95% of executives have said they do not accept cold calls. This should not be a surprise to anyone since in my personal experience of selling for 20 years I have yet to meet a prospect that likes to be a victim of a cold call.

But here is a statistics that any sales executive likes. Survey done by LinkedIn has shown that their members are five times more likely to accept a meeting with someone if they were connected via the network. I work with dozens of sales organizations that have started to reduce their traditional cold calling and instead are using platforms such as twitter, blogging and LinkedIn to identify and approach potential clients.

I have met very successful consultants that market themselves by posting interesting and thought provoking articles relevant to their expertise and have gained thousands of online followers that send in questions, give comments and seek their advice. Guess who they would think of when these followers need the type of services that these consultants are subject matter experts at?

A simple social value formula below sums up why you need to be a true customer advocate and sales professional in the social media age.

Value + social engagement = commercial engagement

"Internalize the Golden Rule of sales that says:
All things being equal, people will do business with,
and refer business to, those people they know,
like and trust."

– Bob Burg

Chapter 4

The Ten Laws of Social Selling

Before I get into the nitty-gritty of your social selling plan, I want to share with you ten universal laws of social selling that will guide you through this lifetime journey.

After working with sales executives and organizations, leaders and business executives, I came up with a list of ten laws of social selling. Before sharing these laws with you, I want to make a few clarifications on these laws:

- They hold true for any country on the planet. It does not matter which city or country you are in.
- Following these laws when you are leveraging the social media to sell will help you to succeed. However, breaking them will cost you credibility, time and resources.

#1 Stop pitching and start connecting

If you break this rule, you will immediately be classified as a sales person and fall into that category of people that almost no one wants to engage. Think, when you connect, follow or friend someone online, what are you hoping for? Probably to expand your network, make your life more interesting, learn, grow and have a better quality of life, right? Last thing you want is to get bombarded with sales pitches.

The whole point of social media is about connecting and engaging people. Rise above and elevate yourself as someone who actually cares about your prospect's business and success. The worst thing you could do is to connect with someone on a social channel, then immediately reach out to them to pitch your products and services. It will only become obvious that you actually don't care about the person and business at all, and that you just want to sell your product. Resist the temptation to follow up with a pitch or a company profile. Just chill! Play cool! Sit back and observe. Read their postings, understand their business and industry, make comments about what they posted and start small dialogs. Start giving value before asking for anything.

#2 It is a journey and not a destination

Once upon a time, when the internet was young and the Web was new, many people thought they will just put up a website and business will start rolling in. Of course, that was not the case then; and it is not the case when it comes to social selling. It is not like you just setup some social channel presence and wait for the business to roll in. Your social media engagement has to be dynamic and ongoing if you want your efforts to be successful and pay dividend on the long run. So, don't think of it as something you do once and then move on.

#3 A. B. C. Always Be Connecting

Seek every opportunity to engage with people you meet and do business with through social media. When you have a conversation with a prospect on the phone or at the coffee shop ask them a simple question "would you mind if I connect with you through –Facebook, Twitter, LinkedIn...etc? you will be amazed how many people will say 'sure'.

#4 Give first before receiving

You know, when you don't feel particularly rich, you're less likely to help others, right? The problem with this approach is that it's a downward spiral. You give less and then you get less. The winning formula here is for you to give and share more than any of your competitors. Build deeper and more engaging dialogs with your prospects and add more value than your partners are willing to do. If your competitors are blasting generic web event invites, you reach out to your key clients to invite them one by one by phone or a personalized email

#5 Steer clear of spamming

Our world and the internet is already flooded with so much unwarranted demand for our attention that we are all tired of it and have become desensitized to it. So, don't make it worst.

The old 80/20 rule applies here. You want to have 80% value add (e.g. shares/postings, comments, likes…) and 20% sales related content. Don't reverse the order. Otherwise people feel spammed and abused.

#6 Be honest

Be yourself because it is a lot easier than trying to be someone else. Don't say and do things that you don't believe in. Because over time the real you will come out and you will lose people's trust. Don't make promises you cannot keep and don't make statements you cannot backup with evidence.

#7 Be consistent

Consistency in your activity is what's going to establish you as a solid source of value. Don't start by doing 10 postings a day and then go down to 2 postings a month. You will lose credibility and followers. As I discuss in your planning stage, commit to what you can and stick with the plan. For example, maybe you do one blog posting a month, and share 3 interesting content on LinkedIn, Facebook, Twitter, and post two pictures a day on Instagram and five twitters a day on topics your target audience cares about and commentary about your favorite team or sports.

Make social media a habit and it will be a lot easier to stick with a plan. Put it in your calendar and try to stick with the plan. Consistency brings you fame, fans and fortune!

#8 Connect and amplify

Build on your network to reach and influence others. Ask yourself 'Do I want a network of one thousand followers That kind of know me, or do I want a network of one hundred people who LOVE who I am, what I do and what I stand for, who will amplify my message to their networks of thousands of people? It is better to build a network of people that know and trust you, and are willing to amplify your personal brand and give you access to their networks.

#9 Use social to get personal!

Social media is not the end; it is the means to get to your ultimate goal of engaging with the prospect. You are simply using the Internet highway to make the drive to your prospect's business faster and more cost-effective. Once you get there through social media, you still want to meet and engage with that prospect; get to know the business and show them how you could bring them value. Every time I connect with someone on LinkedIn or follow them on Twitter, my ultimate goal is to meet or have a video/voice call with them.

Make it a rule to take at least one of your social connections offline and have a live dialog/meeting with them.

#10 Don't forget the 'SELLING' in 'social selling'

I will refer to this over and over again. Don't confuse doing social activities with selling. Using the available social media channels to learn about the prospect and connecting with the right people is all solid activities. But these are all activities that are above the sales funnel (before the prospect is in your sales funnel). You still have to move the prospect into your funnel and ask for commitment to engage with you to progress the opportunity. Without getting engaged and getting commitments from prospects, you are just being friendly and making connections. But you are not selling yet. The selling part happens with you starting to identify challenges, pain points and desires of the prospect that will compel him to take action.

"Without strategy,
        execution is aimless.

Without execution,
        strategy is useless"

– Morris Chang
CEO of TSMC

Chapter 5

Getting started with your Social Media Plan

So far we have talked about what and why. Now let's discuss the 'HOW'. I have conducted, participated and taught thousands of workshops and training sessions in my 20+ years of experience. I have learned that most often, one of the biggest barriers to success is not the intention or effort, but lack of effective planning and execution. First, I like to discuss how to build successful social media program. Later I will be discussing the steps on how to achieve this success. Here, I want to take a step by step approach on how you can become a great social seller and marketer. The approach applies pretty much the same regardless if you are a company wanting to leverage on social networks or an individual who wants to achieve your unique objective through use of social media.

Let's start by looking at your strategy:

STEP 1 – Look at the big picture

Here is where you want to have a notepad, few sheets of paper, bar napkin... available to make notes on. Your social media strategy will have a major impact in your life and business going forward, so don't take it lightly. You need to start by setting higher level strategic goals and then drill down and break those goals into tactical activities and decisions that you will undertake to achieve those objectives.

For this process, I suggest you follow a structured approach. I often use a hierarchical goal setting structure where you start with the high-level goals and then break them down into smaller, more specific actionable goals and activities. Here is a 30 second review of the approach just in case:

HIERARCHICAL GOAL SETTING

Start from the top and set your high-level strategic goal. You need to ask yourself

"What do I want to get out of my social media efforts/investment?"

For this question, you need come up with maximum of three objectives. You may come up with dozens. However, the key to success, as in most things in life, is FOCUS. Trust me, if you could achieve three clearly defined and relevant objectives, you are already a superstar. When I use the word 'YOU' that could be just one person, a department, or a company.

Bring together your team of 1, 2 or more people for some brainstorming session(s) and discuss what you want to get out of your social media efforts and investment. Here are few examples to get you started:

"I want....

- *To increase revenue*
- *To find and attract new clients*
- *To build a new communication channel with my clients or market*

- *Establish myself as a subject matter expert in ......field*
- *To promote my social or personal agenda/values*
- *Make my social media channel as a listening post for your clients and markets*
- *Build a global customer support tool.*
- *To build my brand*
- *Create awareness of a problem, challenge or opportunity...*

This step is extremely critical because it will drive your future decisions on activities, platforms, budget, timeline, and ultimately your long term success. So, "Choose wisely". Later, we will discuss different social media channels and their strengths & weaknesses. I will also cover some of the financial commitments (if any) needed for different channels.

One advice I have is that don't think too hard or make it too complicated. I always say "no good idea ever lasts a committee meeting ☺." Sometimes, when people think too much and too long on a topic, they lose momentum and start thinking of all the reasons why the idea won't work, and then inaction takes over.

One of my favorite sayings on how to succeed with social media is: "MOVE FAST AND BREAK OFTEN." Because this is the best and fastest way to learn and get better.

STEP 2 – Define your success

Once you have your high level objectives set, you need to define what success means. Here are some examples:

I/We define success as

- Having 2,000+ followers on Twitter.
- Getting 100 inquiries a week about our product.
- Having 50 of our regular customers place a lunch. order through our twitter account.
- Have 200 'Likes' for our video postings on Facebook.
- Have 50 people a week sign up for our newsletter or blog.

To get there, you need to set more specific and measurable objectives. A great guide for this is the classic S.M.A.R.T goal setting.

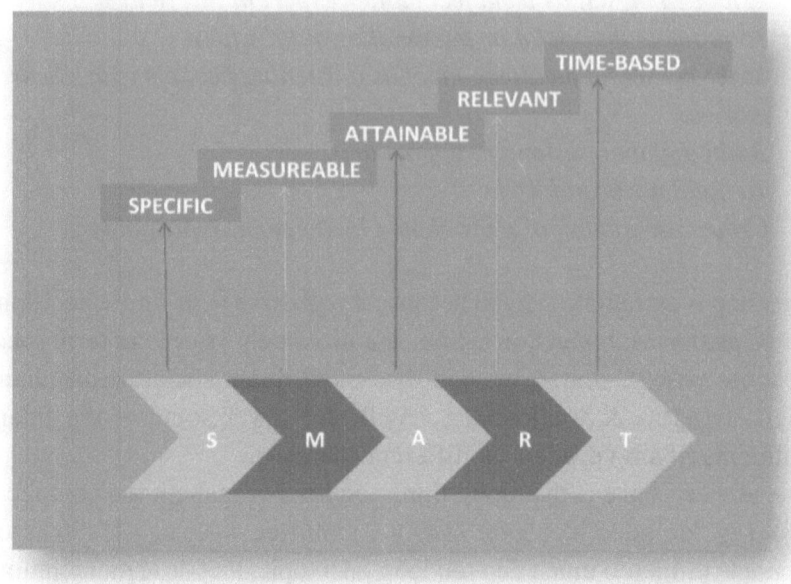

As you are putting in place your SMART objectives, you need to think about how to track and manage these activities. As they say, you can only manage what you can measure. But remember to keep it simple. For example, 'how many new inquiries you get from new prospects this week?' or 'How many people liked and commented on your online survey?". As Leonardo Da Vinci has said, "Simplicity is the ultimate sophistication".

Once you have agreed on your objectives and milestones, you will want to start breaking down the objectives into more real and tangible activities. This means asking yourself "What is it going to take to get 50 people to sign up for My newsletter?", or "What is it going to take to get 50 people to sign up for my newsletter?", or "How would my target audience know that we are here?". How will I market yourself, how often, who would be responsible, and by when? Here is where you break down the activities by months, weeks and days, all rooted in your objectives.

Here are some examples of kind of activities you want to have discussed and documented:

I/We will

- Place 1 article a week on a given topic per week.
- Send out 10 invites per week for new clients.

- Share 2 customer success stories per month on Facebook.
- Read 10 postings of our target audience on our Facebook page and respond to the comments within 1 week.

Here is where you start to realize whether you can do this on your own, or perhaps you will need an external support to help you crystalize your thoughts and ideas; you will definitely need help to execute them effectively. Here is where we often get requests from our clients to step in and support them in this process.

We all have good intentions and don't want to start something if we are not going to succeed. But the reality is that almost all great ideas go bad in the execution phase. It is very easy to set up a Twitter account or a Facebook page. But it seems a lot harder to maintain an updated, dynamic and engaging Twitter account when you have other priorities and activities.

Best advice is to curb your excitement and start with baby steps and keep it realistic. Look at your available time and resources and commit to something you can do in a realistic time schedule, not forgetting that you still have your other commitments in place. You need to have enough activity to be able to get sales traction and see results. Once you start to see real results from your social media activities you will naturally start to prioritize your work.

Do I need help?

When it comes to asking for help, you may be the kind of person who likes to do everything yourself, or you feel that you cannot afford it. Thanks to social media and the internet, there are many places you can go to get inexpensive great help on just this kind of work. There are many service providers where you have freelance writers, designers, programmers and specialists offer their services at very reasonable rates; Feelancer, Guru, Fiverr, Peerhustle and Upwork to name a few. There are tons of very competent, creative and reasonably priced service providers that will do pretty much everything to get you up and running with your social media plan in a very modest budget. I suggest you look at how much your time is worth and make the call accordingly. Is your time better spent talking to customers, managing your business, coming up with the next product, or is it better spent sitting in front of computer for hours and designing your profile or posting blogs?

If you are a sales executive that knows how to use your smartphone and your PC, you are almost sufficiently skilled to execute your own social selling campaigns. At the beginning, you should certainly leverage your manager, colleagues, friends, mentors, spouse, even your kids (my kids know a lot more about social media than I ever could) to come up with your plan and activities. You may consider using the free resources available online or hire a reasonably priced Freelancer to build your social platform profiles, and then take over maintaining them yourself.

As part of your planning, you need to put in place a timeline for achieving the desired objectives and set up regular review times for your strategy (monthly, quarterly, annually) and activities (daily, weekly, monthly), so that you could adjust your plans in case you don't see the results you were hoping for.

The next step is to decide on the platform(s) you are going to use. In the next chapter, I am going to cover the most popular platforms along with some of the smaller and more niche oriented ones.

"Social selling builds on the age-old basics to know your customers and meeting their needs"

– Jon Ferrara

Chapter 6

Deciding on the Right Platforms

There are a lot of great social media tools/apps/platforms out there and they all have their strengths and weaknesses. In this chapter you will read about the major players and their pluses and minuses.

You need to determine which ones work best for you based on your own needs and unique requirements. These days there are social apps and platforms that cater to different profiles such as age groups, gender and personal interests. You may think it's better to join all these platforms, setup a free account and throw a few interesting or cute photos and catch phrases in each one and the business starts to roll in. I wish it were that simple.

The fact is that just as in traditional selling, consistent, long term success comes from hard work, patience, and focus. You need to invest time and energy to put in place the right strategy and then execute on it with clear focus and persistence.

I am going to provide an overview of the top 3 elephants in the social media space and cover the other platforms with their unique characteristics. It is safe to say that if you are working in the Business-to-Business or even Business-to-Consumer space your presence in the top 3 is a must. Now based on the industry, country and segment you are in, you would have a bit of different cocktail mix about where you spend more time and where you hang out more, but you cannot ignore these big social media elephants.

Facebook

Is the undisputed champion in the personal and Business-to-Consumer social media channel. This is the biggest social media platform with over 1.5 billion members worldwide. It has become unanimous with people's digital identity card. Over 70% of adults online use Facebook. Most people use Facebook to connect with friends and family and share photos, ideas and thoughts. Facebook has become the most popular B2C marketing channel in the world with 97% of B2C marketers using it.

It is this personal nature of the channel that makes this platform a MUST for the B2C segment. It is a common approach for many professionals in western countries and elsewhere to use Facebook for their personal connections, friends, families and sharing. But they use LinkedIn for their business profile, connections and engagements.

Interestingly, in many Asian countries Facebook is also considered to be a viable B2B platform. I found out that this is due to the fact that there aren't many strong local business-focused social media platforms and LinkedIn has not yet established itself in the B2B space. In my work across the region I have seen sales executives and small business owners using Facebook for their business and personal communication. If you could manage this effectively, that is fine, but I strongly suggest keeping the personal and professional social channel separate.

Many companies, large and small have been using Facebook as a very cost effective channel to communicate with their target markets. If you are a business, a celebrity, public figure, artist or owner of a unique product Facebook has a very powerful service to help you reach its 1.5 billion members through its Fan Pages.

What is a Fan Page on Facebook, you ask?

A fan page is the only way for businesses and other organizations, celebrities, and political figures to represent themselves on Facebook.

Unlike a personal Facebook profile, fan pages are visible to everybody on the Internet. Anyone on Facebook can connect to and receive updates from a page by becoming a fan (i.e. 'Liking' the page).

Like a friend's profile, Facebook pages allow public figures, authors, businesses and other organizations to create an authentic and public Facebook presence.

But remember that authenticity is at the core of a fan page on Facebook. Just as profiles should represent real people and real names, so too should pages for entities. Only the official representatives of a public figure, business or organization should create a fan page on Facebook.

As a sales organization or a sales executive who wants to leverage the 1.5 billion member strong network of Facebook, having a fan page is a no brainer. The fan page can help you scale yourself and support your clients, prospects, friends, fans and everyone else through an easy to use and professional fan page. Here are some of the key advantages of a fan page: Blog by Kathy Hadley, "15 Reasons/Benefits Of Having A Facebook Fan Page And Not Just a Personal Profile Page For Business", August 8, 2015.

1. Unlimited Friend Count

    While the amount of friends you have on your personal profile page is limited and capped at 5,000, your Fan Page can have an infinite number of fans. This is probably one of the most important reasons that you should be using a Fan Page and not your personal page. Why would you ever want to limit the amount of fans your brand can have?

2. You Have the Option to Keep Your Personal Life Private (-ish)

    In creating a Fan Page you are, essentially, keeping your personal page separate and not connected to it. For those who want to keep Facebook for friends and family, this is an important feature. It's vital. You can control the privacy settings on your personal page and optimize publicity for your Fan Page. It can become incredibly annoying to your friends and family who are constantly seeing business updates from you. This option is a great way around it.

3. Search Engine Results

    Facebook Fan Pages are indexed, which means that some of the public content is indexed as well. As a business, you want to show up on the search engines. Of course, you want to direct traffic to your website first, but having a social presence is very important.

4. Tagging Your Brand

    Your fans and other Fan Pages can tag your Fan Page. Only your friends can tag your personal page. As you want to show up on as many newsfeeds as possible, you definitely want the option to be Tagged in photos and posts by others. This increases your engagement, not to mention your fan base.

5. Facebook Insights

    Facebook Fan Pages have great analytics. You can track the amount of views a post receives and monitor your weekly reach all within the Facebook Insights. To be a smart marketer means knowing how to maximize each post and learning which posts work best for your brand. This is the insight you need to deliver the right content to your fans.

6. Facebook Tabs

    Facebook tabs are only allowed on Fan Pages.

7. Profiles Look like You Don't Know What's Going On

    Plain and simple, a brand that directs to a personal page, just looks amateur. You only get one first impression. You don't want it to be this one.

8. Advertising

    Facebook advertising, while expensive, is very targeted. Advertising to a Fan Page is more effective than an outside landing page because Facebook wants to keep the traffic within the network. You can promote your Fan Page through ads, but not your personal page.

9. Admin Connections

    By granting select people access to your Fan Page, you avoid giving out your password to multiple people. You can choose what rights they get to finagle with and what they can do within your Fan Page. This also allows for a pretty nice check and balances system for your brand.

LinkedIn

LinkedIn is truly a must-have for anybody who is making a living in sales. Frankly, it is more relevant and useful than the CRM systems in some companies. The reason I say this is that the whole point of a CRM system is to bring you closer to your clients and prospects. You can walk into any company and look at their CRM system and be sure that 20% or more of the information about the customer is already outdated for various reasons (e.g. the person left company, phone number, location, business changes… etc). This is the nature of Business as we discussed in chapter 2, CHANGE. However, in most companies nobody is explicitly responsible for keeping the customer data updated all the time, and the realities of business make it almost impossible to maintain an accurate customer database (e.g. Sales people quit, move, change priorities, accounts get reassigned, .. etc.)

But the beautiful thing about LinkedIn is that the members themselves are responsible for keeping their profiles (roles, contacts, company… etc.) updated. And it is to the individual's interest to have an updated profile because he/she does not want to miss out on any opportunities. I have even heard that some people update their profile in LinkedIn with a new job before telling their own spouses! With LinkedIn you have a much better chance of finding the right person and contact information than in your own CRM. Almost all of the sales executives in various companies I know, including myself, go to LinkedIn to validate contacts.

When it comes to Business-to-Business social media channel there isn't anyone even close to LinkedIn for sheer member size, content and focus. Simply put, LinkedIn is a global professional network that allows people to post and share their resume, profile, ideas, services & interests online.

LinkedIn has a network of over 400 million users in over 200 countries. Once in every 2 seconds someone joins LinkedIn somewhere. It is the professional focus of the platform that makes it ideal for B2B engagement and selling. LinkedIn generates more sales pipeline than Twitter, Facebook and Blogs. A survey has shown that if you are connected to someone in LinkedIn, it is 5 times more likely that he/she will accept a meeting request.

It is important to note that HR departments and recruiting companies have been the main consumers of LinkedIn services for years. If you already have a LinkedIn account it is safe to assume that your profile in LinkedIn reads like a resume. Interestingly, I found out that in some countries in Asia the employees are afraid to use LinkedIn at the office because their bosses become nervous and think the employee is job hunting!

LinkedIn Sales Navigator: Over the past few years LinkedIn has gone through a number of major and minor upgrades. What the folks at the company has done is to put some of the most powerful and sales focused functions under their product, Sales Navigator. There is a lot to say about the tool and I run one or two hour workshops to cover all the functionality that you get from the Sales Navigator. Functions such as highly focused filtering, saving leads and following companies and individuals are some of the best functions in this paid version of LinkedIn product. As you probably have seen on their website (www. linkedin.com) They have different packages for different roles and budgets. For most people who want to use LinkedIn as a resume showcase then the free version will probably be all they need. But if you are serious about your career and business, and you are targeting decision makers, executives on more complex selling, then you need to invest in your future by getting the Sales Navigator in one of their business packages.

The LinkedIn Sales Navigator has some great features that are "must haves" for sales professionals. Here are some of the premium features that I think is vital for any professional or business:

- Ability to send out inmails to members (not looking like SPAM email)
- Wide range of filters that allow you to narrow down your searches and search by variables such as industry, company size, title, years of experience & key word searches.
- Ability to find, save and track leads and accounts and receive notices on their online activities. This is a great way to discover 'actionable insight' (basically good business reasons to reach out) about the person you want to reach.
- Ability to set up search alerts and receive notifications automatically.

In short, if you are selling into the B2B space, then you need to invest in the LinkedIn Sales Navigator.

Demand your company paid LinkedIn Sales Navigator

If you are a B2B sales executive and selling products and services that costs more than a few thousand dollars you have every reason to go to your manager and ask for the company to pay for your LinkedIn membership as this is a powerful way for you to build pipeline and sell more for your boss. I have seen many sales executives across the globe who have dramatically increased their sales achievement through the effective use of the LinkedIn service.

Twitter

I have a confession to make. I never cared for Twitter much and didn't see it as a sales tool. But in a span of few months diving in and using it, I have become a 'BELIEVER". Now I know that Twitter is one of the most powerful sales and marketing tools for any business who wants to thrive and grow. Here is why I have fallen in love with Twitter:

Say it in 140 characters: With everyone having an attention span of only a few seconds, Twitter is a great way to target, communicate and engage with your audience. The 140 character limit also forces the authors to get to the point and don't write a novel.

Speaks to the decision makers: The executives, and the decision makers are often heavy twitter users. If you have the right message you are more likely to get through the gatekeepers and the noise to go directly to the boss.

Native mobile: it is made for cell phones and that is where the world is going. Twitter has so much brand equity as the on-the-go social network.

Easy to use: A great feature of Twitter is that you can follow anyone, including your prospects, friends, thought leaders, companies, competitors and celebrities. You could direct your message to a person or to everyone who follows you. You can re-tweet your tweets, which is by itself a great endorsement of the author.

Listening device: Great way to listen to the market talking about you and your brand. It allows for companies to have a very close relationship with their customers by being only a few keystrokes away. It is like a press release at your fingertips.

R&D platform: With Twitter, you don't need to put together focus groups and run surveys to learn what people think about your company and products. Just post a question and let your target audience respond. You want to improve your products or services? Just ask the people that matter to you via Twitter.

Multiplier and soundboard: It is a great way for you to spread the word and lure people to your other sites, blog and commerce site.

Don't forget to visit this book's website to find wealth of resources, tools and ideas on how to better leverage social medial for your business:

www.winningwithsocialselling.com/resources

Many socially savvy companies are using Twitter in very creative ways to build & protect their brand, beat their competitors and sell more. Dell Computer has a team dedicated to using Twitter in generating more revenues. Some airlines have set up teams to monitor air traveler twitters at the airports and look for opportunities to steal away unhappy passengers of the other airlines.

An amazing use of Twitter is that you can go to Twitter and search for a topic of your choice and see what people have said about that topic in chronological order. This is a goldmine for any company looking to serve existing customers and find new ones. Let me give you an example. I was staying at supposedly 4 star hotel in New Delhi recently and I thought the place was absolutely horrible for what I paid for it. I felt so cheated and could not believe that you pay over $200 to stay in a motel 6 looking place. So I got my frustration out by tweeting out about my horrible experience. Within a couple of hours I got a tweet from the hotel chain's customer service apologizing for the experience and asking for the opportunity to set things right. This is an amazing proactive tool to listen to your clients and get in front of murmurs and whispers before they become deafening sound of the stampede of clients leaving you.

Imagine if you sell a CRM software and you search Twitter for key terms around CRM, Needs, Problems..etc. and you will get a list of tweets from people who used those hashtags. Now you have an opportunity to reach out to them and learn what the customer is saying and feeling. Needless to say you check the person's profile in other social media channels to learn more about him/her before contact.

This is a priceless business tool available to you for FREE!

As of now, Twitter has over 250 million users, sending out over 450 million tweets on a daily basis.

Here are more statistic that show the power of Twitter:

Google processes 100 billion search queries per month!
YouTube processes 3 billion search queries per month!
Twitter processes 2.1 billion search queries on a DAILY basis!

Regardless of which channel you are using, you need to consider Twitter as your sounding board and a place where you could promote all your other social contents on a daily basis. Twitter is a way for you to reach more clients.

"Social is not a place for a hard sell —
it's a place to build trust and credibility.
Work the intelligence into your formal sales process
and messaging while staying top of mind by continuing
to interact on a personal level over social media."

– Julio Viskovich

Chapter 7

Other Major Social Media Platforms

After the major 3 players I covered earlier, there are a few other social media players that you should know about as each one has its unique benefits that may make it a viable tool in executing your social media strategy.

Google+

Needless of what you say about its popularity, this platform is supported by one of today's largest companies in the world with the technological and financial support that not many competitors could match. Many compare Google+ to Facebook as the way it works and its target audience. But Google+ has some advantages that Facebook cannot match. For example Google+, as you would expect, is fully integrated with Google's other products. It also comes with a feature called "hangouts" which are video conference calls. You can also email anyone that includes you in a circle. Google+ does not have as many users as Facebook, but with its powerful brand and more focus on business users it is a platform that you should stay on top of. Google+ has over 540 million users.

YouTube

Owned by Google, it is the 'go to' site to post and view the wide range of videos online. If you want to maximize viewership you have to include YouTube in your social media strategy. For businesses using YouTube is a smart choice as it makes it very cost effective to instantly make your content available to billions of people. Many small and large companies use YouTube to educate the general public, their customers, even their own employees. This is a great way to communicate your products and services benefits through the most consumable form. Of course you need to make sure to create decent quality videos. If you are comfortable in shooting videos or have a team who could do that for you it is worth considering YouTube as a key pillar in your social media strategy. I have seen people and companies from all industries and backgrounds promote their business and expertise through this channel.

Remember that today's consumers are smart and technology savvy. One of the most effective ways to make new clients is to educate them. YouTube allows you to do that in a personable and easy to use format. They don't have to read a 50 page white paper to know you are a subject matter expert. A good customer story video of 2 to 3 minutes could relay the same message to your target audience.

YouTube is also a great tool for you to watch and learn about your customer. See a video that your potential customer has posted about their business and what matters to them. Use it to highlight what they do well and align your products and services with what they do and how they could do it better.

YouTube has over 1 billion visitors each month and there are over 6 billion hours of videos are watched each month.

Instagram

This is a powerful photo and video sharing platform. Facebook bought the company in 2012. You can post images, use filters to enhance the look, 'like' images and build network of friends. I suggest looking up some of your clients and see what they are sharing on this platform. To see someone's postings you have to know their username and the account has to be a public. If the person set the account to Private, then you cannot see their postings unless they grant you access. Of course brands and other public figures have public accounts. You can also comment on other postings and start a dialog. In some cases based on your industry and your client's profile Instagram can help you to learn more and your client and better engage. However, a large portion of this platform's users are teenagers, making it more ideal for companies that cater to this age group.

I know my son and daughter use it on their cell on a daily basis and put in comments, forward pictures to friends and 'like' dozens of photos before I could pour my cup of coffee.

Instagram has over 200 million users.

Blogging

Blogging has been around for a long time and even if you are not into social media, I am sure you have read a blog or two on your topic of choice. Blogs are a powerful tool to make yourself known to your target audience, build your brand, build trust and build a business. Especially if what you have is knowledge and expertise blogging is a great way to stand out among the crowd. I cannot imagine someone making a living as a subject matter expert and not having a blog of their own.

Blogs are also a great way for you to learn about your target clients. Many people in prominent positions have blogs where they share their thoughts or ideas. If you are trying to break into an account make sure to see if any of the leaders have a blog and make sure to read their blogs to learn about their priorities, values and preferences. It could save you a lot of time in finding their hot buttons and building the right strategy.

What is great about blogging is that anyone could write one. Even you! If you enjoy writing and like to share your knowledge with the world start to write your own blog. But, before doing that, make sure you spend a few days thinking and planning your blog strategy. Consider how much time you can spare per week to write your blog, read and respond to other people's comments.

Make an agreement with yourself about how much time you will dedicate to the task per week or per month, and stick with it. You are doing this to build yourself up as an innovator, subject matter expert and professional. The last thing you want is to have your potential client to go to your blog posting and see it was last updated a year ago. It doesn't build confidence.

What I found to be a practical and doable schedule is to do a posting once every two weeks or once a month depending on your industry and trade, supplemented by other activities including retweeting, comments on relevant sites and social groups, and sharing beneficial links, articles and videos on major social channels.

The good and bad thing about blogs is that you can write as little or as much as you like. So be careful not to get carried away and write up a novel that no one has the time or patience to read. Also, don't post something that is so light and fluffy that the reader finds it a waste of time and reduces the chance of the visitor returning to your page.

I would also strongly recommend keeping separate blogs for your personal vs. professional topics. Some people have strong social and political points of view and like to let the world know about them. However, your personal values and stands are not something you want to mix with your professional profile as it may turn off people who may not agree with your personal stands.

Now, how do you choose?

I already discussed some of the main social media platforms and their strengths/weaknesses. The next decision you have to make is which social media channels you should be active on? The answer is of course where your target customers hang out. As I talked about this topic before, it doesn't matter which social media channel you find interesting or useful for you; the important thing is which ones your customer uses.

Image 7-01 shows the global monthly active users for top media platforms.

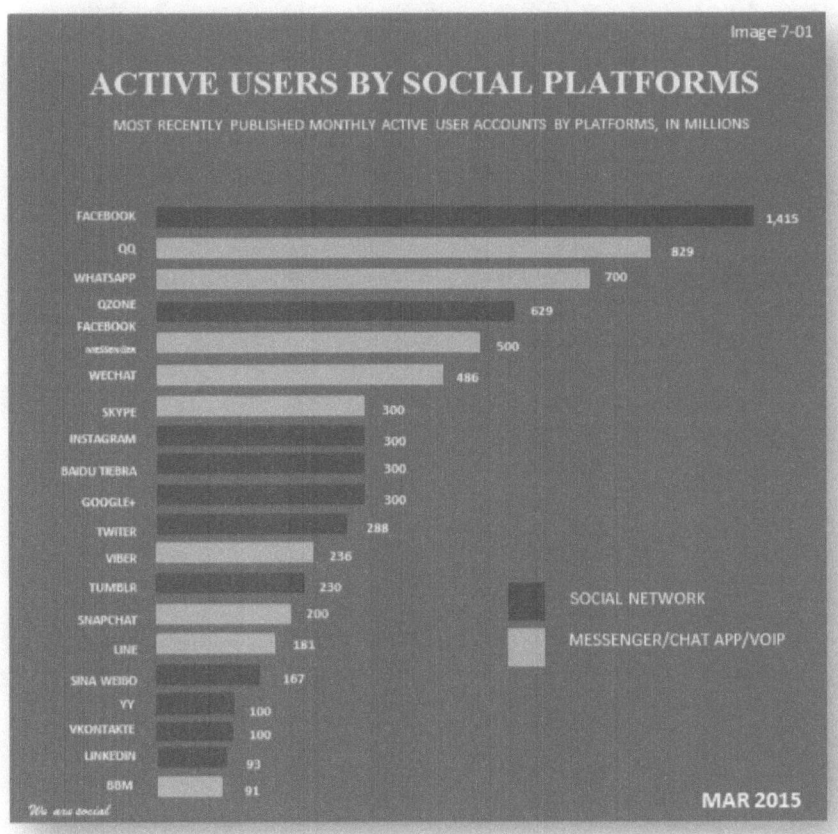

Image 7-01

ACTIVE USERS BY SOCIAL PLATFORMS

MOST RECENTLY PUBLISHED MONTHLY ACTIVE USER ACCOUNTS BY PLATFORMS, IN MILLIONS

FACEBOOK	1,415
QQ	829
WHATSAPP	700
QZONE	629
FACEBOOK messenger	500
WECHAT	486
SKYPE	300
INSTAGRAM	300
BAIDU TIEBRA	300
GOOGLE+	300
TWITER	288
VIBER	236
TUMBLR	230
SNAPCHAT	200
LINE	181
SINA WEIBO	167
YY	100
VKONTAKTE	100
LINKEDIN	93
BBM	91

SOCIAL NETWORK

MESSENGER/CHAT APP/VOIP

We are social

MAR 2015

I want to point out the volume of social media active users for Asia Pacific is over one billion users, of which around 90% of them are using their mobile phones to access their favorite social media platform.

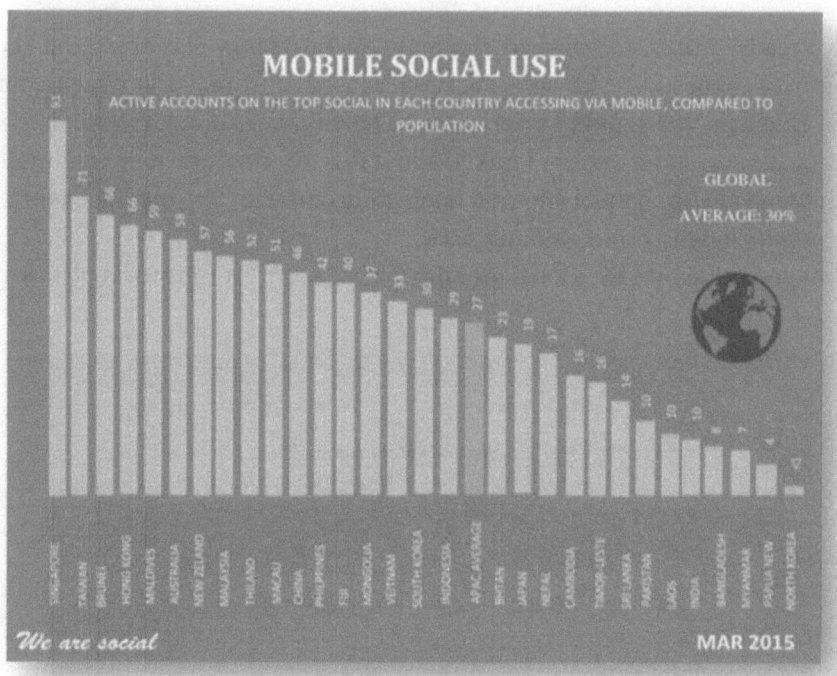

*Sellers who've embraced social media are
creating new opportunities that totally bypass
traditional sales channels...
It's about good selling – using all the tools that
are available to you today."*

– Jill Konrath

Chapter 8

What it takes to win with Social Selling

In Chapter nine, I will share with you the 3 steps in becoming a social selling success. But before that I want to share with you what I (along with many of the leaders in the industry) believe to be the key principals of effective social selling strategy and execution.

You still have to SELL

I hear some social selling advocates say that you no longer need to do cold calling and doing demand generation activities of the past. Frankly, I have found that some of the people who advocate these views have never actually carried a sales quota. They say that you just connect with people and start to have conversations. Then sooner or later sales will just happen. Well, I wish the life of a sales executive was that easy. Yes, social media, used properly, is an incredible tool to engage with people. See the diagram below, showing a typical sales funnel.

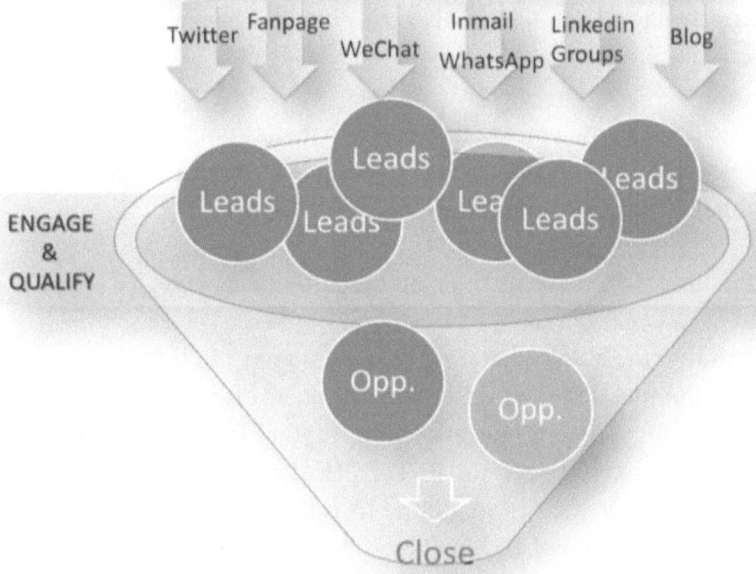

As you see your social selling activities are all happening above the sales funnel, before you get the prospect into your pipeline. The connection and conversation is only half of the selling. Once you have identified interest you still need to engage and do a traditional qualification of the opportunity. This process of qualifying and asking for commitment to continue with the business engagement is the other very important part of selling and it is something that often cannot happen over Twitters or Inmails.

Social selling has dramatically improved your ability to identify and reach out to the right people. But you still have to build rapport, show value, build trust and get the decision maker(s) to sign on the dotted line (these days often digitally).

Be a celebrity!

In this super busy and celebrity crazy society of ours, you need to be your own biggest promoter, every day, everywhere and using every relevant channel possible. You need to build your brand as a subject matter expert, as someone who adds value, and someone that your target client should talk to when they require your product, service or expertise. This is only achieved if you are there and you can be reached. To be clear, if you are not seeing good Return On Investment from your social media activities, it is because of one of these two reasons:

- People don't know you are there (which means you are not a celebrity)
- People have forgotten you (which means you are not present in the right channels frequently enough to stay top-of-mind)

…Or of course the third reason could be both the above ☹

The solution to the above challenge is that you have to be an active player in every social channel that your customers are at, as often as possible, adding value and promoting yourself. Doesn't matter if you like the channel or not; if your customer is there, you need to BE THERE. Doesn't matter which social media channel is your favorite medium. In other words, "your customer's favorite social media channel is your favorite social media channel". For the Millennial generation you have to be in the social channels that they are using. If you are selling to young professionals you need to see which channels they are using. Of course you need to consider the country and the region as well.

Becoming a celebrity could do wonders for your business. But you also need to consider what kind of celebrity you want to be. One major mistake that most of us sales executives make in our social media face is that we position ourselves as the best/most successful/experienced/overachieving Sales person! What? Unless you are looking for a new job, why would you announce to the world that you are a (Great/Amazing/awesome/superstar… etc) sales person? Why do you want to promote yourself as a sales executive?

Tell me, when was the last time that you got excited when you got a call from a sales person you don't know who wants to sell you something that you don't think you need? Do you like to talk to sales people? Does anyone on the planet like talking to a sales person that he/she doesn't know when he/she does not have a need? Then why would you position yourself as a sales person that 'crushes' his/her quota every time? How would a customer feel when he/she reads that you are a super successful sales executive? Perhaps a little scared and extra guarded?

Yes, it is fine to say you are great at your job in your resume and when you are job hunting. It is not good when you are trying to get people to open up to you and have a dialog.

Follow these steps to narrow down how you should position yourself or your company:

1- Think about your target prospects and ideal clients. Then consider what are some of their challenges that you could help them with. For example:

   - Small businesses don't have the skills & resources to figure out which social media strategies and tools would make them more successful.
   - Labor costs keep rising and companies are looking for ways to reduce their cost of raw material to offset the increase.
   - Inventory management is a big challenge for smaller manufacturers.

2- Think about, and decide what are the top 2 to 3 values you or your company could provide for your target clients. Here are some examples:

   - I help my clients to increase revenue through effective digital marketing programs.
   - My company helps small businesses save 20% on raw material cost by sourcing from overseas vendors.
   - We help companies manage their inventory better by using real time inventory systems.

Consider, what are the messages/words/stories/proof points your target audience (with the identified needs in step 1) will be looking for? Then build your messaging aligned with these points.

   - For example share stories on how you have helped companies with similar challenges to achieve their goals.
   - Share research from known authorities that support your approach.
   - Offer fresh and different ways to look at an old problem and challenge the target client to question the status quo

Give, Give, Give, then Ask

Some of the questions I get from business owners and sales executives are "is it ok to pitch in my social engagements?" "how much and how often I should be selling? "When should I ask for the business?"

These are great questions and here I want to talk about what is the best way to start your engagement and strike a balance between being social and being a seller. First, I like to go on a little rant about how every time there is a new tool that can help you build your business, the marketers and novice sales professionals quickly destroy its effectiveness and turn its novelty to nuisance by abusing it. Remember, just 10 or 15 years ago when you got a spam from a vendor? (Which wasn't every 5 seconds), you actually read it! Here are some figures that show how the abuse of digital marketing tools has destroyed their effectiveness:

Year	email open rates	Banner ad click-thru rate	cost-per-click demand for Google adwords 2011 to 2012
2002	37.30%	3.00%	
2009	26%	0.50%	
2011	1700%	0.10%	Down 15% y.O.Y

The point is that we have all become desensitized and cynical about anyone approaching us for any reason. Even if you send a genuine and worthy prize to 1000 people in an email, it is likely that 995 of them will delete it without even reading it. People see through your scheme very quickly and will shut you down. So the answer to the question is "should I be pitching?" Is "Yes, but not from the first engagement." One of the great books I read on the topic of digital marketing is *"Jab, Jab, Jab, Right hook"* from one of the social media gurus of our time, Gary Vaynerchuk. In his book he explains that in today's crazy busy world where everyone is out of time and patience you cannot get far by pitching. The best way to engage with your customers is to give, give, give, and then ask. In other words, give something that they would be interested in; something that adds value in their eyes. Then you earn the right for asking for their attention.

The concept of earning the 'right' to ask for something is critical in any sales process. We don't live in the pre-internet & pre-information society world where just saying that you are from IBM or General Motors or Proctor & Gamble would earn you the right to take up a prospect's time. In today's consumer dominated world you have to earn the right to take up a decision maker's time, every time.

The first thing you have to do is to make yourself relevant to the person you are trying to reach. It is about your messaging and how your message gets the person to read on.

You may say "but Mark, I sell xyz product or service and don't think I can give much except information about my company or product". This is where you need to think as they say '...outside the box' (I know, this phrase is getting old ☹). Here I share with you a simple and effective way you could do this, for FREE! ☺.

Let me ask you to do an exercise. Nothing that will break a sweat, I hope. Take out your cell phone and flip through your screens. Think about all the apps you have on your cell phone and try to separate them by their theme and general purpose. I am not looking at your phone with you right now, but engaging my telepathic powers I could guess that your apps would fall into one these 3 categories:

1- Social networks apps that help you stay in touch with others, which means you are interested in other people.
2- Entertainment, such as games, music to help you unwind and escape.
3- Tools & utilities such as organizers, calendar, email, and exercise trackers to help you become more efficient and have a better quality of life.

So if these are three possible areas you care about it is likely that you would be open to hear about one of these topics, right? So think about your product or service and think how it helps your target audience in one or more of these areas. For example, if you are making cupcakes your message could be around how your delicious & healthy cupcakes will help people to enjoy a guilt-free break from their busy day. If you sell super comfortable shoes, your message could touch on studies that have shown comfortable shoes reduce long term fatigue and back pain, reducing your medical bills. If you are providing massage service in the business district, you could share scientific studies that talk about many benefits of short nap in productivity and mental health.

When you are using social media your 'give' could be light content that aligns with one of the three areas and provides a benefit to your target audience by making them laugh, ponder, play a game, feel good, feel appreciated, or just help them escape for a few seconds from their stressful day.

The great thing about being a sales executive in this era of social media is that now you can find out so much about your target audience before you even deliver your first 'give', making it hundred times more effective since it is customized. You could look at your target customers' postings, profile and comments, to better understand his/her likes & dislikes. You can then customize your value and messaging around that.

Social media is changing the way we communicate and the way we are perceived, both positively and negatively. Every time you post a photo, or update your status, you are contributing to your own digital footprint and personal brand.

– Amy Jo Martin

Chapter 9

Three Steps to Higher Social Media Enlightenment
(Build you profile)

After helping hundreds of professionals build and execute their social media success plan I have put together a simple and easy to follow 3 step process to execute your social media strategy.

First STEP: Build your profile

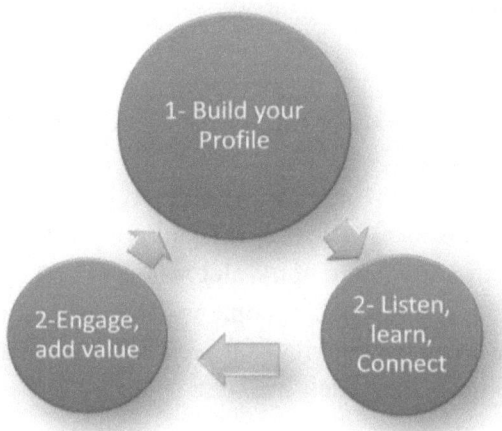

Regardless of which social media platforms you use to improve your revenue potential the first step is to start building the right image for yourself and your business. Remember that your social presence has the potential to be viewed by billions of people around the globe; often times their first impression of you, therefore you want them to have the best first impression.

Your profile is also a major part of your BRAND, especially at the beginning, before your other attributes such as professionalism; customer service quality, expertise, & character have established and solidified your brand.

There is a lot that goes into building the right profile. Some of the social media platforms such as LinkedIn and Facebook allow for more comprehensive and customizable profiles with lots of control over what you can do and who can see what; While others have a less complex structure with limited features. But regardless of the platform, you need to build a profile that is:

- Authentic
- Positive & exciting
- Interesting, attractive & visual
- Unambiguous
- Professional
- Aligned with your objectives
- Relevant to your target audience

In this chapter I will give details and tips on building the right profile for some of the more mature and function-rich social platforms, namely Facebook, LinkedIn and Twitter. However, the above principals remain valid regardless of the social site you use.

But first let me explain a bit about each of the above principles.

Authentic: It goes without saying that you need to be honest and by yourself. Don't try to be someone else as it is very difficult for you to maintain an image of someone or something you are not. Value who and what you are and build on it. The fact is that sooner or later people who engage with you will see the 'real' you and if there is a gap in what you say and who you are, then you will lose trust and more than likely their business.

Positive: Of course by being honest I don't mean to say that you cannot put a positive spin to your strengths and capabilities. Just as any company would, you want to highlight how you have helped others, what you can do for your target audience and your core beliefs so that people will see who they are doing business with. In your profile you have to focus on positive themes and how you can help others to reach their objectives. Use positive and energizing words that move people to imagine, aspire and act.

Interesting & attractive: Do everything you can to make your profile more interesting for the viewer. 'Interesting' comes from many different elements, including what you say, how you say it, esthetics of your profile page and even the font you use. So try different combinations (keeping in mind your target audience) and find elements that makes your profile more interesting.

Here are some of the elements I recommend my clients to use in their profile:

- Make it as interactive as possible. Ask for opinions, call to action and propose a new way of looking at the world.
- Use multimedia content, not just text. Use images, videos to engage quickly (again consider the target audience)
- Tell a story; don't just state facts and figures. Stories engage and provoke emotions.
- Point out what is unique about you and your business.
- Use a layout that is easy to read and intuitive. Don't overuse hyperlinks and colored fonts, prioritize content from left to right and top to bottom as most people digest information this way.
- Be aware of the font you are using and avoid making your profile too crowded.
- Use high quality, high resolution videos and images.
- Consider the fact that the majority of people use smart phones for viewing social media. Therefore, you need to be aware of the screen size and layout.

Unambiguous: don't confuse people with poor writing skills. Have a few colleagues, employees, friends, family members you trust to review the profile and give you feedback. I recommend this to my clients that if you can, pull up your profile on the computer, tablet or smart phone and give it to your colleague or friend to view and watch how they react. You can see how their eyes move and the expression on their faces. It says a lot about how effective your profile is.

A major pet peeve of mine that drives me crazy when I review people's profiles is usage of jargon, technical terms, internal words and downright fluffy words that means nothing. Please consider who is reading your profile. More than likely they never worked in your company or department and have no idea about your internal lingo. Avoid putting words and phrases that are put out by people who get paid for making up words to confuse people. In addition, remember that many words and phrases mean different things in different industries, companies and even cultures. Again, have an extra pair of eyes review your profile and ask them to question any word or phrase they don't understand.

Professional: needless to say once you have posted something on social media you pretty much have no idea who is going to see it. Therefore, you want to make your first impression a good one. Build a profile that looks and feels as if a professional marketing agency built it. Your narrative has to be a professional one without coming across as being insensitive, unprofessional or a jerk. Be careful about using humor as it could backfire as different cultures see and interpret it differently. It seems like a no-brainer, but make sure that you have included how people can reach you and your company.

Aligned with your objectives: Your profile structure and theme needs to be aligned with your objectives. Again, this seems to be a no-brainer, but I see so many profiles of people who are trying to build a business as an independent consultant but their profile in social media looks like a job resume. I have advised hundreds of executives and sales leaders on how to start viewing their social media presence not as a job seeker but as a thought leader and influencer. So if your objective is to find new clients in new markets or countries your profile should showcase success stories and innovative ideas that will be relevant to those markets.

Relevant to your target audience: As much as you may think it is a good idea to be all things to all people, the reality of our modern world is that no business or person can do that. Your social media profile should speak to your target audience. If your objective is to reach out to IT and technology leaders then your profile wording, your background, stories and the content you are using should be speaking to technology people. But if you are targeting the Accounting professionals your profile will have to resonate with them, using terms and wording that resonates with them. In case you feel that you have two or more very different target markets you are going after, I would suggest that you either have to make your profile more generic so that it would resonate with more people, or try to identify if there are shared values among those various target markets that you could speak to without alienating the others.

Your TOP THREE social profiles

The above profile guidelines that I just provided, should apply to any public profile you may have. But now I am going to discuss building the right profile in the top 3 social media platforms, namely Facebook, LinkedIn and Twitter.

Your Facebook Profile

Here are 5 tips on how to make a great Facebook profile:

#1 Create an eye catching and compelling PIC & cover photo. This forms your visual identity in Facebook. Your profile photo is one of the most important aspects of creating your identity on Facebook. It is visible and it is your 'face' on Facebook.

You want the image to be interesting, professional, high quality and aligned with your values. To see examples of high quality and very popular Facebook pages please visit our website www.winningwithsocialselling.com/resources/samplefacebookpages

You want to make sure that your images are:

-   Aligned with your goals and target audience
-   High quality and leave an impression of quality and professionalism
-   Are consistent across your various channels in message and quality.

Here are some tips on getting the right images that help your business.

1. Style and tone

Decide what you want your page to convey.

-   Prefer a more personal, informal tone? A photo of you would be great.

Remember to stay consistent throughout your page(s).

2. Dimensions

- Your profile pic will be displayed as a square. Keep this in mind when designing your profile picture. Don't upload a rectangle as this will get cropped and may cut your image.
- Facebook recommends that you upload an image that is at least 180X180 px, though the display size of your photo will be smaller.
- Your photo is displayed at different sizes at various places. As of last year the Facebook business page layout guide is:

  - The main image on your page: 160X160 px
  - Next to posts on your timeline and in the news feed of fans: 40X40 px
  - Next to comments: 32X32 px

So use images that look good when displayed at the smallest size. Remember not to use small text in your image. It may become so small that is not legible.

Note: since social platforms upgrade and change their designs it is always best to check the relevant social media platform for the latest guidelines.

3. Quality

- Upload a high quality photo or it may appear blurred.
- Make sure your color contrasts work. Don't use a dark background for a dark logo.

4. Consistency

- Use the same profile pic across social channels for brand recognition. One caveat here is that if you are going after a wide range of target clients in age, country or background, you may need to have multiple versions of your photo to match the medium. Having a business suit may not connect well if you are targeting teenagers.
- Try not to change your profile pic too often as this will affect brand recognition.

5. *Visible area*

Your profile photo will hide a part of your cover image. Design your cover photo so that no important piece of information gets hidden.

Facebook has recently added a dark gray gradient to the bottom of the cover photo and action buttons for 'like', 'follow' and 'message' towards the bottom right corner. Keep in mind that these can also interfere with your cover photo. For instance, don't put your shop name or website where they may get hidden by the buttons.

6. *Identity*

-   If it is relevant, use your cover photo to tell visitors what you do. It makes it easier for the visitors to quickly understand what you do by looking at the images. Of course for some products it is easier to do this than others.

Try to get a vanity URL. You want your Facebook address to be unique, easy to remember and inviting. What you don't want is some random characters and symbols as Facebook will give you automatically when you setup an account

Which one is easier to remember?
This one?
facebook.com/marksmith3215/123456%&(*^
Or this one?
facebook.com/winningwithsocialselling

A good url should be:

•   Short
•   Have your company name
•   No extra characters & symbols

Facebook automatically adds some numbers and characters to your url when you create a business page. You may think that you are stuck with that. But actually you can change it and make it more user friendly. There are easy instructions on how to change it on the Facebook website along with hundreds of other sites.

Keep in mind that as of now, Facebook only lets you change the URL address once.

Get the word out

You may have the best solution in the world and the most amazing Facebook site, but it will do very little if nobody ever knows you are there. You need to actively promote your Facebook page and all other social media sites.

Make sure you:

- Add your url to your email signature, business cards and other material.
- Get active on other Facebook pages and groups.
- Invite friends, colleagues, clients, and acquaintances to visit your page.
- Ask your happy clients to add testimonials and comments.
- "Like" your page.
- Cross promote your site with your other channels, and if you are a business, with other complementary businesses that you could collaborate with and have a shared interest.

Create and update engaging content on a regular basis

Building a Facebook page and having some comments up is pretty easy. The hard part is maintaining your site fresh and inviting. You need to add the contents of all your social media sites on a regular basis if you want to continue to build and maintain visitor traffic.

Read the chapter on Social Media tools for a host of new tools that can help you keep all your social media channels in synch and updated.

Get help

If you haven't already, you will soon realize that maintaining an exciting and lively social site is not easy. Let's not forget you have to still do all your other work that you did before you bought this book and uncovered your purpose in life. This is why I often suggest to my clients to get help from friends, colleagues, and professionals. These days there are a lot of freelance service providers that can help you build and maintain a vibrant social presence at very reasonable prices.

Your LinkedIn Profile

When it comes to B2B, LinkedIn certainly is the most effective social media tool. LinkedIn's profile allows for a great deal of functionality to showcase your skills and expertise I really like the amount of flexibility you have in creating a sales focused profile.

Here are 10 tips you can do today to make your LinkedIn profile a powerful selling engine:

TIP 1: Your profile is for your customer, not you!

Don't write a profile from your point of view.
Look through your target customer's eyes.

When you are building or reviewing your profile stop and think about your ideal customer, his/her industry, job title, possible challenges and what are the key words and phrases he/she will be looking for if he is looking for the expertise/solutions/products that you offer? Then start building a profile that highlights those key points and values.
You want to attract the attention of your target audience, so think about what they are looking for.

TIP 2: Upload a professional photo

Profiles with photos are **14 times** more likely to be viewed than those without (source: LinkedIn).

Include a professional headshot of yourself that would be worthy of a business card. Profiles with photos receive a 40% higher InMail response rate because people like to see who they're speaking to. Think of how you would want to appear in a face-to-face sales call or professional networking event and upload the appropriate photo.

LinkedIn conducted a number of surveys tracking the eye movement of the people opening LinkedIn profiles and tracked where the viewers are looking at the most. Here is what they found out:

Dark circles represent the more viewed sections of the profile. As you can see the two most viewed areas in a profile are the photo and the job title/description

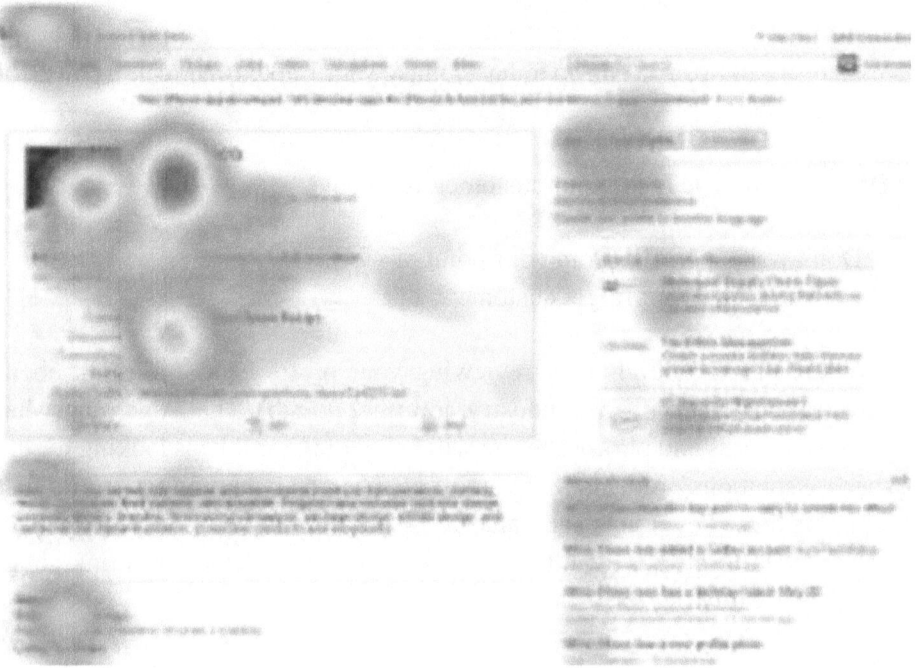

What this means is that viewers look at the photos and titles. If interesting, they will scroll down and read more. If not, they move on. Keep in mind this often happens within less than 2 seconds.

TIP 3: Write an easy to understand title and compelling headline

Job Title: My first advice is don't put your job title if you are a sales person. Nobody wants to talk to sales people. Your job title should be 'What's in it for your target clients'. Write something that will get your target client excited and call you. If you want to write a job title, make it easy enough that most people could understand. Avoid super fancy titles that confuse people. Here are just some sample titles that leave people scratching their heads (at least for me) and wondering exactly what you do:

Assistant improvement program manager
Finance quality vice-president.
Public Happy Maker
Virtual World Developer
Center for Excellence VP

Title, description: most people do not realize that in the space assigned to the job title of your LinkedIn profile you can add a sentence that will allow you to further explain what you do at your job. This has a number of powerful benefits. It allows you to explain your value in business terms from the customer perspective. For example, how many people are tempted to call you just because your title is 'Sales Executive'? I am sure probably not that many. But what if you can explain in a sentence that you "help CFO's in the chemical industry to save on procurement expenses by up to xx%"?

Mark Ghaderi 1st • PREMIUM
Author | International sales trainer | Speaker: Helping Asia's most innovative and successful compaines to achieve their vision and aspirations

Send a message   View in Sales Navigator

https://eg.linkedin.com/in/mark.ghaderi   Contact info

TM

Another important benefit of the headline is its search ability. When you put in key words commonly used by clients to seek out people with your skill set, having those phrases in the headline increases your search engine ranking. So that by using keywords, you are more likely to show up closer to the top of the search results.

Again, it is important for you to put yourself in your target customer's shoes and come up with phrases that they would be using in seeking out people with your skill sets.

TIP 4: Allow easy access

I mentioned this tip while discussing your Facebook profile. With LinkedIn, as in Facebook, when you first setup your profile the site assigns you a URL that you can share with others to view your profile. You can add this URL to your email signatures, business cards, social postings and other places to attract more viewers. However, by default the automatically generated URL may not be so easy to remember or share. But you can go into your profile setting and try to find an easier to remember URL. You could include your company name and your name in your URL.

Don't forget to put your contact information in the profile. Certainly your business email and contact number are critical. Once you've connected with a prospect or colleague, you'll want to make it easy for them to contact you. Add your company email address and phone number at a minimum. Your contact information is only visible to your direct connections.

TIP 5: Build a resource, not a resume

This is one of the biggest problems I see with almost 95% of the profiles I have been asked to review. They all look like they were built to help the person get a job and not a customer. I find the profiles of sales people, especially loaded with hyperbole and bragging about what a great sales person they are and how they crush their quota every month, quarter or year. This kind of pitch does not give you much credibility in the eye of your target customer, unless they want to hire you. So, once you have a job, you need to sit down and look at your resume as your target client would look at it and see what they want to see. What resources you can add to make your profile a resource that they can come to and learn something they didn't know before that actually helps their business.

You certainly can add links to resources, write short stories that tell how you helped other companies to increase revenue, or reduce costs or have happier clients.

TIP 6: Add Rich Media

As I mentioned at the beginning of the chapter on your profile you want to make your profile more interesting with easy to consume content. Multimedia content such as videos, SlideShare and photos make your profile look more lively and interesting. In your LinkedIn profile one more place where prospects and customers can access and download important files and presentations such as data sheets, white papers, and presentations. Upload files from your computer or add links to videos and SlideShare presentations to display your own presentations, and check out presentations from your colleagues. Look for the Add Media button in the Summary, Education, and Experience sections of your profile.

TIP 7: Tell your story in your summary

The person's summary is one of the most viewed areas after the photo and heading. Write a story about yourself and how you have helped other businesses to be successful.

At the end of your summary make sure you have a call to action. Ask the viewer to do something such as "if you want to learn more about how you could do XYZ, drop me a note" or ask them to view the video you have posted.

TIP 8: Update your current and past positions

Put a little detail about what you have done in previous companies. I often see people just put the company name and date of start and finish. This does not say much about what you have done and learned there. Again, show how you have impacted your employer and your clients. just one or two well written paragraphs from your customer point of view.

TIP 9: Add your education, other certifications and general topics of interest (the more the better)

I recommend that you share as much information about yourself as you feel comfortable sharing. For example mention if you are involved in some charity work, community activities or sports.

As you may know, the LinkedIn search engine is continuously searching for commonalities and areas of shared interests among its hundreds of millions of members. When you run a search in LinkedIn, you may have noticed that on the right side of the profiles you view, there is a box that shows what you have in common with that person. For example, if you have shared interests, employments, schools and sports. By sharing more about your background and interests, you are increasing the chances of having more in common with the people you are searching for and this in turn provides you with more topics of common interests to discuss.

As you know building rapport in sales is critical to your success and by having more shared topics there are more opportunities for dialog and building rapport.

You want to mention the schools you have attended as this will allow you to tap into your alumni connections to help grow your network, leading to better chances for future opportunities. This also makes it easier for your former classmates to find you as well.

If you have done company sponsored trainings and certifications you want to include them in your profile.

TIP 10: Ask for recommendations

Make sure to ask for recommendations from your colleagues, bosses, and companies you have worked with. However, recommendations from current and past clients are even more valuable. Showing that you have helped others is best way to build trust and beat the other guys.

When asking for recommendations to be specific and focus on specific skills or personality trait that drives their opinion of you. I had an account executive of a vendor who was applying for an internal job in her company ask me for recommendations on traits and skills like "leadership", "negotiation" and "customer focus".

When you are making recommendations make meaningful comments About the person (how you describe others and your experience with them says as much about you as who you are recommending). Think quality, not quantity, and be authentic.

How to get more recommendations

I often hear people tell me that when they ask for recommendations they seldom get a response back. To add to the anxiety, they say they feel reluctant to follow up and ask again.

Here is a simple technique that will dramatically increase your chances of getting the recommendations you deserve:

Write what you want them to say about you and send it to them! You may be thinking this looks like cheating or somehow not right; it is not. Let me tell you why this is a great practice.

What do you think when someone asks you for a recommendation? Do you automatically know what to say and how to say it? I am pretty sure your answer is "NO".

Well, this is how others feel when they get your request. The fact is that people seldom know what to say in a recommendation. Let's face it, people are very busy these days and they cannot take days thinking about what to say and they may not feel comfortable asking you what you want. So your recommendation request just sits there and after a while is forgotten.

Here is how you solve this problem: YOU WRITE THE RECOMMENDATION! And send to them, asking them to edit it as they see fit. Follow these easy steps:

1- Write one or two paragraphs (keep it short and to the point) what you want them to say about you.
2- Email it to them and ask them to edit it as they see fit and send back if they are comfortable. Make sure to give at least a soft deadline, so it won't linger. Below is a simple example that you could edit and use as you see fit.
3- After you get the recommendation make sure to thank them and offer to give them a recommendation if they ever need one.

"Hi xxxxx,

I am building up my social media (name the channel if necessary) and would really appreciate if you could give me a recommendation. To make it easier I have written a draft recommendation that I like please read and see if you are comfortable with it. Please edit it as you see fit and send back to me. I appreciate if you could respond within the next week. Thank you in advance for your support and please don't hesitate to ask if you would like me to write a recommendation for you.

Regards,
Mark"

Try this and you will be amazed by the response.

Your Twitter profile

By now you know the core principals of building an effective profile on social media. The key elements of good profile will apply just the same to your Twitter profile. However, your twitter profile is much simpler than the work you have done with your Facebook and LinkedIn profile. As we discussed if you already have built contents and graphics you want to re-use them for your Twitter page because this will help you build a seamless and consistent image, making it easier for your target audience to recognize and connect with you.

Your profile shows the world who you are. This is the entry point for your Twitter visitors, so make it a good one.

Here are the fundamental components of your Twitter profile page and how you can maximize their impact:

1. @username

    Your @username, also known as your handle, is your business's unique identifier on Twitter. It should be 15 characters or less and should be easy to remember. Whenever possible, make sure your company name is embedded into your username.

2. Profile photo

    Choose a photo that visually represents your business and fits well in a small space. This image isn't just on your profile page; it will be shown as the icon in every Tweet you post. Choose something that is instantly recognizable. Logos work, but you can also feature a person or character.

    Recommended image size: 400x400 pixels.

    Use a GIF or PNG. As we said, stay consistent and use the same images you used in your other social platforms.

3. Your Bio

    You have 160 characters to tell your story with a clear, concise bio that describes your business, products or services. Tell people why your business is unique and why they should follow you. You could also add useful information such as your operating hours and location.

4. URL

    Make it really easy for potential customers to find your website by including a trackable link.

    Again, stay consistent with your other digital sites such as your website, LinkedIn and Facebook profiles.

5. Header image

    Get extra creative with your header and showcase your business with a large, rich image. You could feature products or services, or you could edit the image to include copy which highlights a special sale or promotion.

    Recommended size: 1500x500 pixels. The image is automatically resized to fit.

    Note that the header photo is cropped to a 2:1 aspect ratio for mobile.

    Always review your profile page on mobile as well as desktop. It can look different and with many Twitter users accessing the platform through their mobile devices it's important that it works across different platforms.

6. Pinned Tweet, Use this feature to get maximum exposure at the top of your profile timeline for your best Tweets. Click on the "more" option on the Tweet you want to pin and select "Pin to your profile page."

Building your network

If you have been living on planet earth for the past few years I am sure you already have at least a Facebook, Twitter, LinkedIn, Whatsapp, Google+... etc. account(s) to keep up with the family and friends, find a job, find a friend or a date. For more and more people the social media channels have become their primary place for conversation and engagement with others. A number of surveys have shown that in some communities an average time spend on a single social platform is more than four hours, which pretty much takes up most of the free time people have each day.

For most people a large portion of the time they spend online is spent on building and maintaining one's social network. People spend a lot of time seeking and connecting to others so that they have more connections/friends & followers. I know many people who are obsessed with their ever increasing presence and network size. So much so that the size of the network/friends/followers/tags has become a status symbol and a sign of legitimacy and social popularity and acceptance. There are many businesses that will sell you Twitter followers or Facebook friends by the hundreds or thousands if you so desire.

Let's talk about your social network and what is the best approach in building your network of virtual friends, groups and associates.

I am sure you have seen people on social networks that have thousands of virtual friends and in some cases millions of followers. What do these numbers mean and should you be worried about how to get connected to thousands of people.

In almost every social selling workshop I do, I get asked the question: "should I accept people's requests to connect or be friends, even if I don't know them?" Or "should I connect to people that I don't know?" Well, if you are a sales professional and want to use the social media sites to increase your revenue potential the answer is NO. You do not want to connect with people just for the sake of increasing your connection ticker. There is no value in having a link to someone when the link is too weak to leverage for starting an engagement.

Let me give you an example. Say you are at a trade show and someone you never met before sees your name badge and calls you out by your name and asks for an appointment. Would you grant their wish? I would guess probably not. He hasn't established much rapport or value for you to gain your commitment. There is no benefit in having a network of 1000 people that have no personal connection with you and don't know you from any other human being on earth (except having clicked on the accept button, often without even reading your name).

The point about having connection and the size of your network is quality and not quantity. Take your time to build the right network.

The best practice is to only send an invite to someone you already have had some contact through calls, events, online exchanges, meetings or groups.

Do not accept invites to join the network of people you have never met or communicated with. Connecting with people you don't know makes for a weak link that you cannot build your future on.

If you get an invite from an unknown person, just reject it. Don't worry; they will not get a rejection notice on the platforms that I know of.

Think about what people are doing on Facebook today. They're keeping up with their friends and family, but they're also building an image and identity for themselves, which in a sense is their brand. They're connecting with the audience that they want to connect to. It's almost a disadvantage if you're not on it now.

– Mark Zuckerberg

Chapter 10

Three Steps to Higher Social Media Enlightenment
(Listen)

Listen

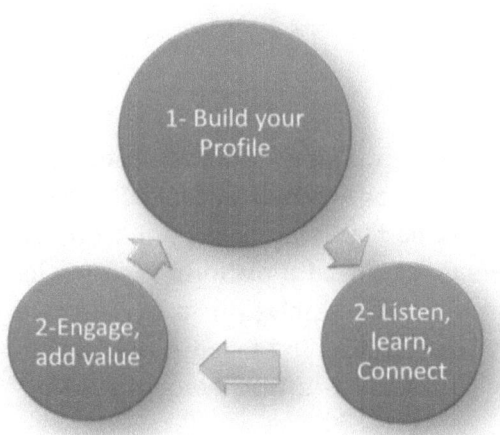

One of the key assets of the best sales professionals regardless of digital or analog world is their listening skills. Becoming a social champion starts by listening to your target audience & customers, identifying what they are really saying and asking for, and then adding value by offering more of what they are interested in. The social media has created a super easy and universally accessible platform for sellers to connect and listen to millions of voices of the consumers and engage with more intelligence.

But there is a catch; you need to be serious about hearing what people have to say and acting on it. Don't just hear what you want to hear and don't just give lip service to repeating what people are telling you and still deliver what you want to deliver.

Where to start

When I help sales teams to get on the social selling track usually after the first stage of getting themselves established on the relevant platforms, I work with them to set up their listening channels on different platforms based on their unique social media strategy. Where you are going to go to hear from your target audience depends on which segment of the market you are operating. Are you targeting the B2C or B2B market? are you specialized by industry or Line Of Business? Are you after consumers with certain profile (e.g. age group, gender, financial status,…etc.)? For example if you are in the fashion industry, going after the young adults and teens then you would be watching Instagram, Pinterest, or Snap. If you are after a bit older crowd for fashion, Facebook plays a bigger role.

LinkedIn

For those of you who are working in the B2B space then you definitely want to be using all of the services available in LinkedIn to connect and listen to your clientele. One of the best listening posts at LinkedIn is their Groups. There are thousands of groups in LinkedIn platform based on industry, profession, company, country and other variables. In fact, you could join the existing groups or make your own groups. In LinkedIn, you can join up to 50 groups. I recommend to my clients to use up all 50 groups allowed.

If you are wondering which groups you should join, here is the best practice:

- **Clients**: start with your clients. Look up the profiles of around 10 clients that you want to engage with. See which groups they belong to. If you are targeting specific job titles such as CFOs, CEOs, or COOs, then you will find quickly that many of these people are members of very similar (if not the same) groups; especially when you get country or region specific.

- **Prospects**: Look at the accounts that you want to get into and then look up the titles that you want to reach in those companies. Again, look up a handful of those contacts and see which groups they are a member of. Then join those groups.
- **Industry / LOB/country**: you can search the LinkedIn groups and identify groups that are specific to the way you work. For example, you may be selling to a specific office such as 'office of CIO'. You could search for CIO specific groups and join the ones that are more likely to include your target client based on topics, industry or geography.
if you are selling to a specific industry such as Healthcare or telco, then you want to be listening in and aligning your messages accordingly. Then you should identify such groups and join them on LinkedIn.
- **Competitors**: as the old saying goes "keep your friends close, and your enemies closer." Don't forget your competitors. You want to also see where your competitors are and make sure you keep tabs on them. You want to look up your competitor firms and see where their top leaders are on LinkedIn and pick a few groups to join. If your competitors are bigger companies, you will find that there are hundreds or even thousands of company specific groups on LinkedIn which will allow you to listen to what they are talking about.

What to do next

You may wonder now that you have joined these groups then what? What should you do next? Here is what you should be doing. Make it a habit of going to your groups at least twice a week. each time pick just 3 or 4 groups to focus on. Try to keep track of this so you don't spend too much time on one group while ignoring others. Remember, you want to be a celebrity, always present. The more you appear in front of the audience the more valuable you become – like the Kardashians!

Read the top three most popular or most recent discussion posts and look at the discussion owners and their profiles. Who are they? What is their background? Could they help you with your objectives? See if you have a strong feeling about the topic or something valuable to contribute. You want to listen for:

- Industry or role specific language/jargon
- Common challenges and problem areas that get mentioned by multiple people.

- Look for people posting questions or asking for recommendations on specific problems or solutions. I have seen so many companies ask for advice on a particular solution or looking for vendor recommendations.

Word of caution: don't start to jump in by pitching and dropping product names and asking for appointments. Continue to listen to the voices and start to identify people and other groups that you may want to be more engaged with.

Chapter 11

Three Steps to Higher Social Media Enlightenment
(Engage)

Get Engaged

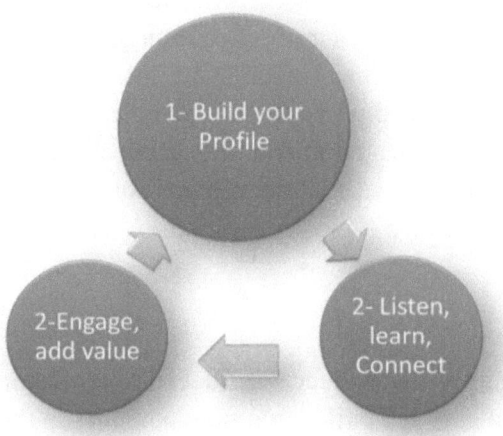

The next step in your social journey is to start engaging people and groups through social media. You already have the right profile, you already are an active listener, connected with your target audience, knowing what they are interested in and more importantly you know where you could add value to their lives. Now you want to start to have two way communication with the audience. Here are basic rules of effective engagement. You may think they are too basic, but believe me, many people don't seem to follow these basic guidelines:

- **Be respectful**: be sensitive and respectful of what others are sharing and saying. Do not discourage and attack others since you don't know their specific background or situation.
- **Be yourself**: don't try to please everyone and say what you think different people want to hear. You cannot keep it up long, and people will see through it pretty quickly, damaging your personal brand.
- **Add value:** Try to add a new angle, a view, fresh perspective, or just your honest opinion in every exchange and engagement. Don't just deliver fluff. As I discussed in chapter 8 give value, give value, give value, then ask for something.
- **Be consistent**: don't start by doing 5 postings a day and in a few weeks go down to one a month. Manage your time and resource and set the audience's expectations by doing something regularly but consistently. What I am talking here is basically having discipline in your work.

The best way to engage is to observe what people are saying and what they are looking for, and then you start to share your thoughts, comments, and value. What I recommend to my clients is to allocate at least one hour twice a week to scan the platforms they are active on and add at least 3 postings in each one. Of course you may adjust that number based on the channel. For example, you may write an original article and share it on your blog once a month. But then you could easily twitter on 5 topics in 5 minutes.

Success stories

I have had a number of very successful social sellers come up with creative ways to help their clients and build large sales pipelines in the process. Here is what one of my students did after she attended one of my sessions she joined a number of LinkedIn groups in her target industry within the manufacturing sector and she identified 2 common problem areas that seemed to be shared by the manufacturers in South East Asia. She then initiated 2 activities that she managed over 4 weeks.

First, she posted a question in the groups that said something to the effect that "I am seeing many of my clients not being able to find the right source of raw material that is dependable and consistent in quality. Does anyone else have the same challenge?...". within days she had dozens of supply chain and COOs put comments and complain about similar challenges.

She read the participants' comments and picked the top 3 most interesting comments and reached out to them with some personalized feedback and comments which led to a couple of conversations and having meetings to further discuss the topic. She ended up having 2 opportunities from this single (free of charge) activity.

The second activity she did was to post a very simple and non-threatening survey, asking the participants to answer a multiple choice question. The survey asked, "which one of these three challenges do you have in your business and what are you doing about them?" A great advantage of using surveys is that the human brain is wired to answer questions. So if you ask your brain a question, it is bound to give you an answer. The sales executive got over a half a dozen promising responses and started to engage with the individuals, building a very healthy and pre-qualified (people already said they had those problems) pipeline within a month!

The moral of the above story is that in today's super-fast super convenient digital world, you don't need a lot of money. You just need good ideas and then executing them with passion and focus.

Make sure to visit:

www.winningwithsocialselling.com and go to the section "resources" where you will find a lot of additional tips and resources that will ensure your online success; the catch is you have to DO IT!

Go to the link www.winningwithsocialselling.com/resources and download the "90-day social selling plan for busy sales executives" that puts you on the path to be a social selling pro right away.

Chapter 12

Getting Social in Asia Pacific

As of 2015 the Asia-Pacific region accounts for more than 50% of all social media users worldwide. Indeed, Asia has become critical to any social media company with aspirations to greatness. Over 426 million monthly active users of Facebook are in Asia, and around one-third of all Twitter users are found within the Asia-Pacific region countries.

A staggering 97.3 percent of social network users in the region access social media channels on their mobile devices, spending between two and four hours each and every day on those platforms.

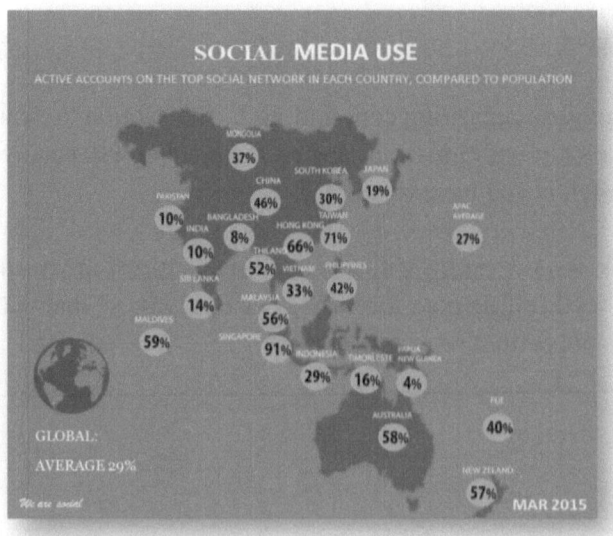

The vast memberships and fast growth show that social media is a truly global phenomenon. Most of the major social networks have global audiences numbering in the high millions, if not billions, with growth in nearly every country around the globe. Social media channels can connect you to billions of people thousands of miles away with a few keystrokes, instantly! As a sales professional, and hopefully one that wants to be the best at what you do, this is an unprecedented opportunity to do what your predecessors could only dream of just a few years ago.

Despite all the closeness an Internet connection can provide, there are still some fascinating behavioral patterns that mark the borders between regions and countries. When you are doing business across borders, it is important to understand how different areas of the world view and use social media.

Asia Pacific is a particularly interesting region, with generally high rates of Internet usage and a range of social networks that are unfamiliar to western audiences. Understanding the ins and outs that distinguish these markets is a must for large & small companies alike who are looking to engage, build rapport and do business.

Broad Trends in Asia Pacific

A study by integrated communications agency <u>Waggener Edstrom</u> examined brand engagement trends within the broader Asia-Pacific region as well as in specific countries. The research found that 78 percent of consumers get information about products and services on social media, and 68 percent share that brand-related information on social channels.

Here, I will review the social media use in Asia's key markets, and typical behaviors for social media use in these markets. For each market you will see 2 charts with first one giving you a market size overview and the second chart showing you the social media channel ranking by the number of users.

Australia

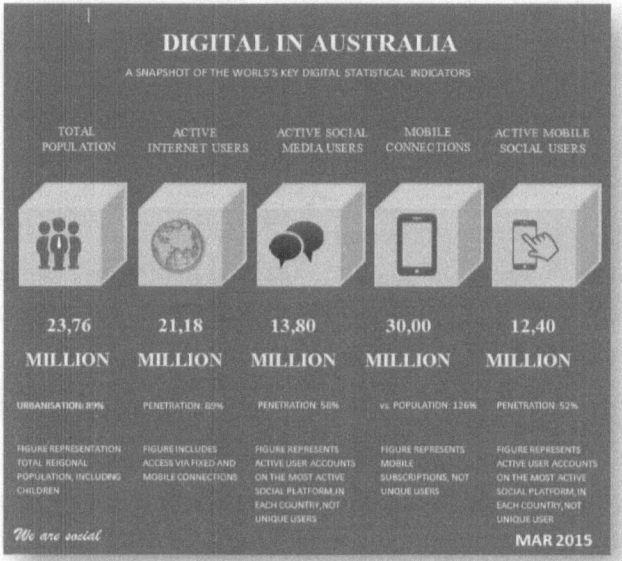

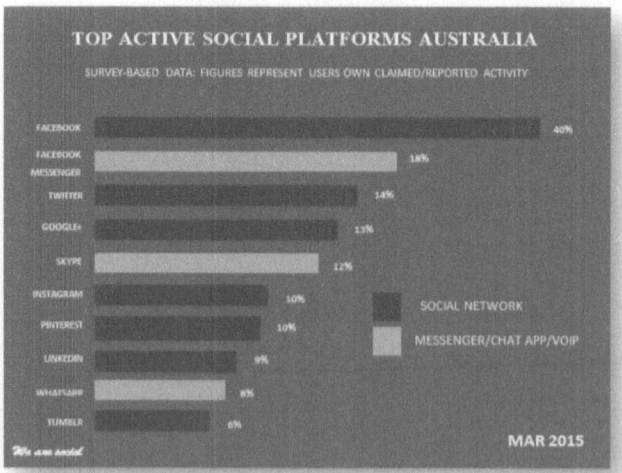

Australia is a mature market with good infrastructure and well-connected population. A majority of the population is using two or more social media platforms to stay in touch with friends, family and the rest of the world. For the B2B space, LinkedIn is certainly very popular, reportedly with over 7 million members. For prospecting and selling LinkedIn is perhaps the best route. Many sales organizations in large and mid-size companies have been leveraging the social media quite well and are no longer questioning if the approach works or not. I know numerous sales champions in the Australian market who have been very effective in surpassing their sales targets consistently, with more than 50% of their pipeline coming exclusively through their social media activities.

If you are selling or managing sales teams in the ANZ market in a B2B environment you should consider signing up for one of LinkedIn's paid services as you cannot do a lot of targeted sales & marketing activities with the free version of the service.

Your other best friend in the Australian market is Twitter. It is the most popular messaging platform for business, and you can do a lot with this channel to offer your products and services. Even if you are a small mom & pop shop running a retail store or a cafe, I see almost every cafe in the downtown area having a sign in front with the Twitter handle asking people to follow them, check their offers and tweet their orders in.

Of course if you are in the B2C market then Facebook, Google+, Pinterest & Instagram presence are a must.

China

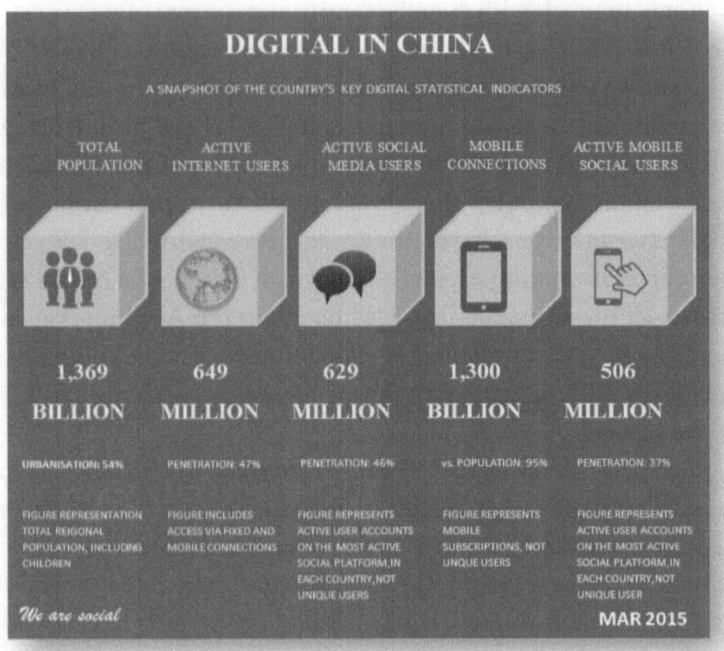

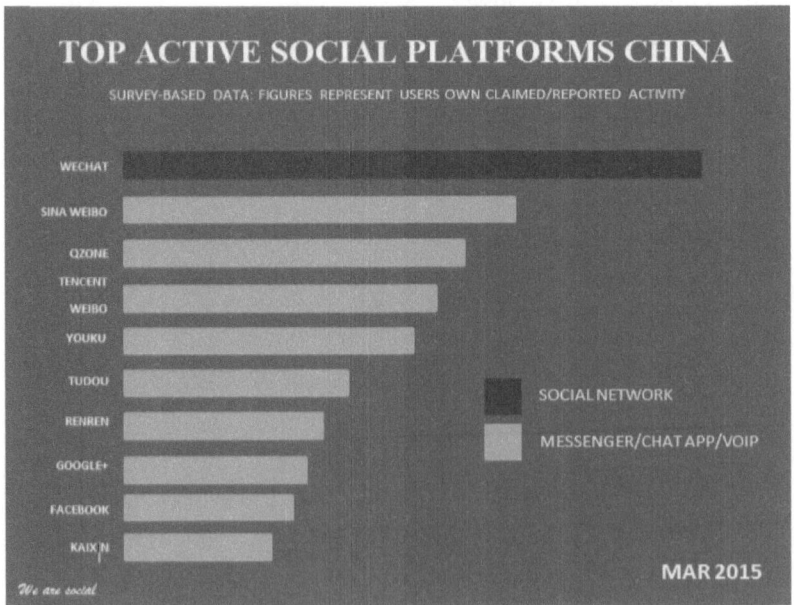

China is one of the most interesting nations in this region. The world's most populous country has some restrictions around web properties; in fact, some of the top networks in other nations are blocked entirely. That's not to say social media is non-existent. Statista projected that there would be 410.5 million social users by the end of 2015, rising up to 504.1 million in 2018, and We Are Social found social media penetration at 42 percent of the total population.

The primary use of social media channels in China is to stay close and communicate with friends and family. Using social media for business has not really taken off in China mainland.

It's important to note that to expand its presence in China, LinkedIn launched a Simplified-Chinese language site and setup partnership with Sequoia China and China Broadband Capital. With this partnership, LinkedIn is hoping to dramatically improve its presence and popularity in China.

Rather than Facebook or Twitter, Chinese netizens are more likely to be on networks created by Chinese businesses. Conglomerate Tencent owns several social media properties that have huge followings. Messaging app QQ ranked as the second most popular network in Asia Pacific with 816 million users.

I travel to China almost every month and just over the last two years I have seen a number of trends (backed up with some recent studies) that you should be aware of if you are selling in china.

- More and more people consume videos on their smartphones. In fact the statistics show that the Chinese are spending less time watching TV, instead opting to watch their videos and TV shows online. Every time I get on a train in Beijing, Shanghai or other major cities I could attest to that. Of course, the internet infrastructure in the major cities are much better and allow for this trend.
- Studies have shown that the Chinese consumers spend more on the brands that they follow online.
- Today's Chinese consumers are extremely brand conscious. The Chinese consumers are now the world's number 1 buyers of luxury goods. But even though they are into brands, at the same time they have much less loyalty to a particular brand and are more likely to switch brands based on the latest trends or recommendations from friends.
- The Chinese rely heavily on peer reviews. Actually research has shown that they write and act on, online reviews of products and services far

more than westerners do. So this means when doing business in China you want to make happy customers and have them support you by giving you online recommendations and testimonials.

- Messenger apps have been very innovative in providing new services to their users, allowing for commerce to take place using their expanding array of services. WeChat, which boasts being the most popular social platform in China, along many others in the same space, are offering money transfers and payment services.

India

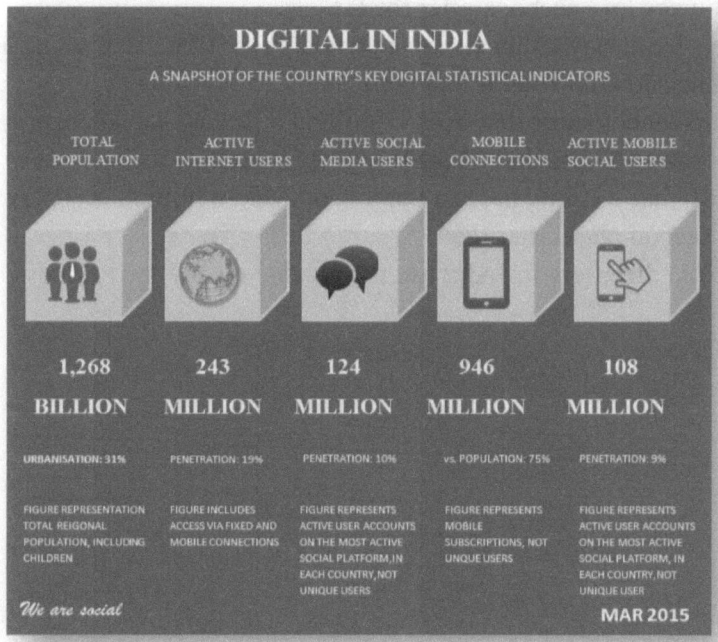

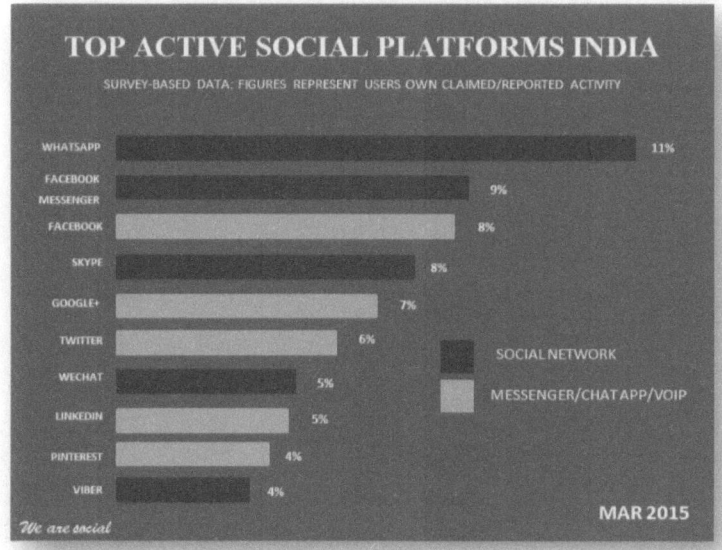

India has over 135 million active social media users as of August 2015. Facebook has over 130 million (94% of social users) user base, second largest number of users for Facebook after the U.S.

Surveys have shown that the most popular reason for using social media is to stay connected with friends and families.

It is important to note that over 97 million of India's social users are using mobile phones to access their favorite social platform.

LinkedIn has a strong base in India with over 30 million registered users, putting in second place after the U.S.

The LinkedIn users in India use the service mostly for business and job search.

Indonesia

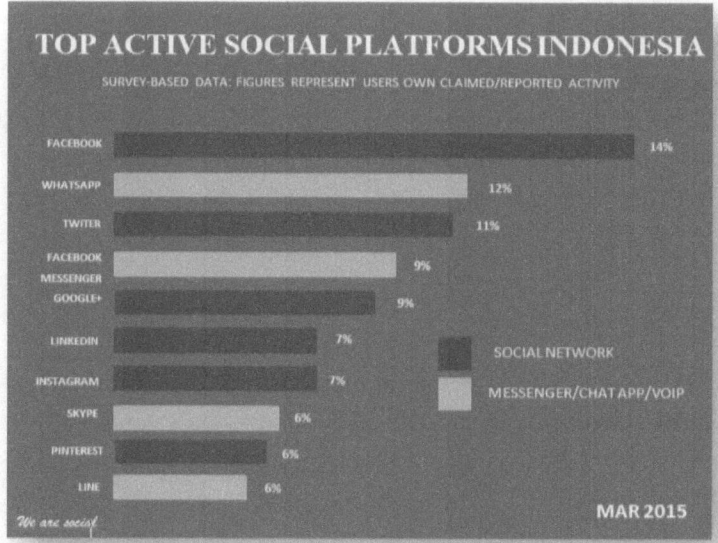

We now look at the fourth most populous nation in the world, Indonesia. Here's what the country looks like in numbers.

- 72.7 million active internet users (sadly that's 0 percent growth from 2014)
- 72 million active social media accounts, 62 million of which are mobile users
- 308.2 million mobile connections, 99 percent of which are prepaid users

When taking a deeper look into what has happened in the past year, you'll see that 50 percent of all online activity in Indonesia is done on mobile. Laptops and desktops account for 45 percent of the activity while tablets get only 4 percent of the action.

Internet use is almost synonymous with social media use in Indonesia, according to February 2015 polling by Asosiasi Penyelenggara Jasa Internet Indonesia (APJII). Using social networks was the most common digital activity conducted in the country, and beat out browsing and searching for information by nearly 20 percentage points among internet users

As for the most popular social networks in Indonesia, Facebook, Twitter, and Google Plus top the list. Interestingly, although Indonesia has become the main market for Path, the report suggests that Instagram and Pinterest are still more popular than the private social network.

When looking at the internet and social media use by age Indonesia has a quite skewed curve. APJII investigated Indonesia's internet user population demographics and characteristics as well as its preferred activities. Just under half (49.0%) of the internet population in the country was between 18 and 25 years old, with another 33.8% ages 26 to 35. That means more than eight in 10 internet users in Indonesia were under age 36.

Messaging is king:

Indonesia has shown its appetite for messaging apps on their cell phones. It may seem quite a feat for Jakarta to be named the world's number one "Twitter city," considering it is the capital of a developing nation in which only a quarter of the population has access to the internet at home.

Indonesians are some of the most active users of messaging and chat apps in the world, with an average of 4.2 messaging apps installed on their smartphones.

Messaging apps are also a significant part of their everyday behavior. 97% of mobile users in Indonesia access messaging apps multiple times per day and 39% prefer them as their main channel of mobile communication over SMS, social networking, voice messages, and emails.

The top three messaging apps in Indonesia are:

BBM (BlackBerry Messenger)
Line
Facebook messenger

Establishing a strong social media following has now become crucial for both local and international companies who want to do business in Indonesia. To be successful in selling you have to leverage the top 3 social messaging platforms and establish yourself as a thought leader and value provider.

Japan

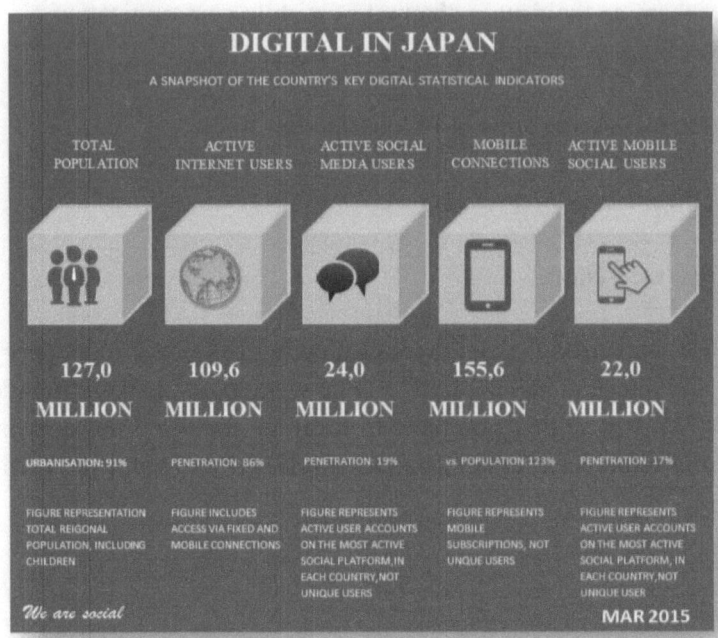

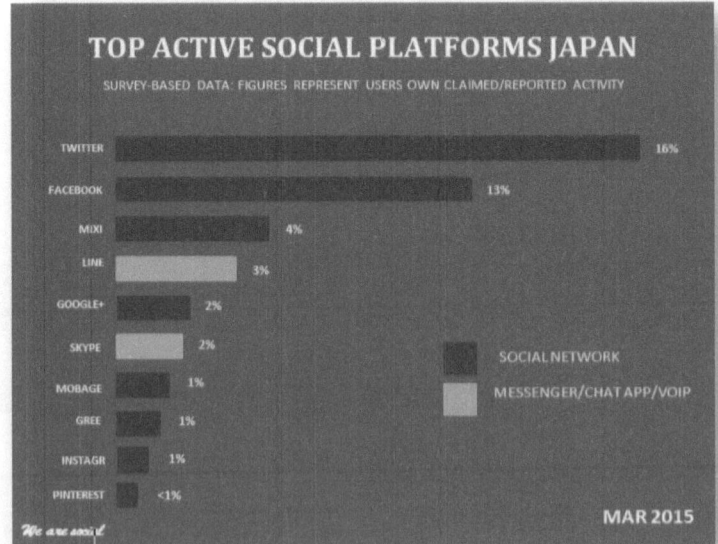

The cultural values of a society have a huge impact on how a country would use social media. Japan is a great example of how its cultural values have kept the adoption of some social media platforms (such as Facebook and LinkedIn) quite low. For instance, the Japanese culture highly discourages self-promotion and boasting Therefore building a self-promoting LinkedIn or Facebook profile will not do much for your social life in Japan.

Japanese do not feel comfortable sharing their photos and details online. This is one of the reasons Facebook is not enjoying a great deal of growth in Japan. Ironically because Facebook's policy for members to use their real names, some companies and individuals in Japan use Facebook for business.

LinkedIn has a relatively small user base in Japan and for the most part the company's main activity in that market is around its traditional recruiting services. The small percentage of the population who knows LinkedIn, they pretty much see it as a job hunting tool. In fact earlier this year when I was in Japan for a social selling event a Japanese employee claimed that he cannot use LinkedIn at his company because of the fear that his manager will think he is looking for another job.

Twitter is very popular in Japan. In fact, it is the second largest market only after the U.S. There are a number of reasons why Twitter has been successful in Japan.

- Japan has been a leader in mobile networks with cell phones becoming the main way for people to communicate.
- It is considered rude in Japan to talk on your cell phone. In fact, if you get into any public transportation and a lot of buildings they have announcements and signs to discourage you from talking on your cell. Therefore the Japanese have become more used to texting for communication while they are spending hours in the public transportation system to commute.
- You can say a lot more in 144 Japanese characters than in English. The Japanese use the Kanji characters (same as the Chinese), and one single Kanji character could mean a whole word or phrase in English.

An interesting difference in the way Japanese use the social media channels vs. the western markets. The Japanese use the social media channels to socialize rather than to share the news. An evidence of this is that only 4% of Japanese Tweets use hashtags (#)

Malaysia

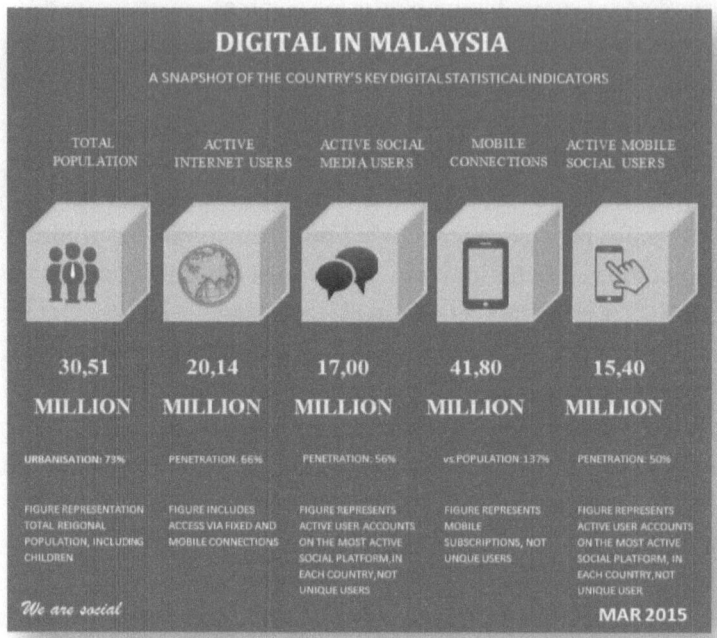

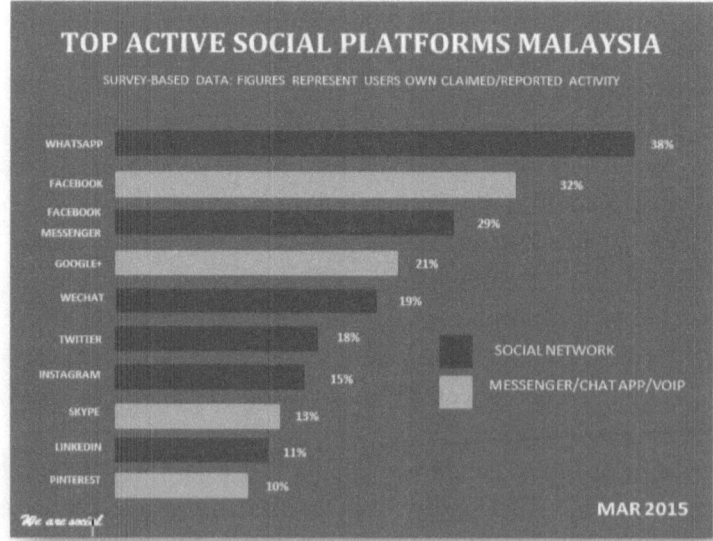

With close to 19 million users online, Malaysia has a social media penetration of 64 percent, which is considered one of the highest in this region—second only to Singapore. Marketers view the social media landscape in Malaysia as vibrant, with most of the Malaysian population turning to social media platforms to have their voices heard.

Apart from advocating social awareness, we are also seeing an increasing number of Malaysians making use of social media in their purchasing decisions. Findings from a recent survey by Adobe suggested that as much as 70 percent of Malaysians turn to brands' social media platforms to research and find out more about the products before making a purchase. This is evident as top Facebook pages tracked in Malaysia were found to be of consumer brands such as McDonald's, KFC, Head and Shoulders, Visa, etc.

Malaysia is embracing mobile commerce in a big way, with expectations of the industry to make up almost 60 percent of the total e-commerce market by this year. Messaging chat apps like LINE and WeChat will be a big driver of this trend, as the country has also established itself as one of the highest adopter of such messaging chat apps. LINE, for instance, has reached 10 million users in Malaysia mid last year, and WeChat tracked a 95 percent smartphone penetration rate with Malaysian users in May this year.

These messaging apps have also evolved beyond their basic functions of just mobile messaging to become more interactive social media platforms for brands to engage with their customers directly on a more personal level. For example, LINE Shopping Malaysia, which was launched two years ago, has already partnered with retail brands, such as Rakuten, Groupon, Lazada, and ZALORA. As for WeChat, they have been working with brands in Malaysia such as ChaTime and Domino's Pizza to extend deals and rewards to their users.

Singapore

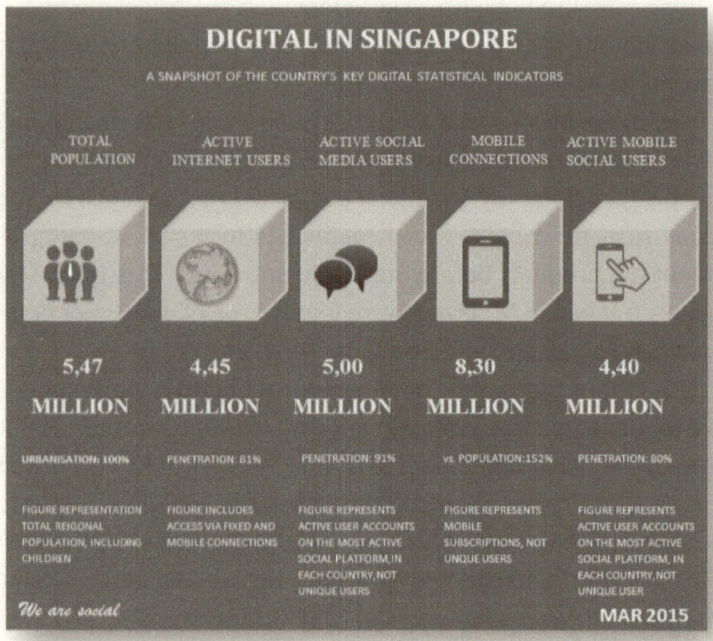

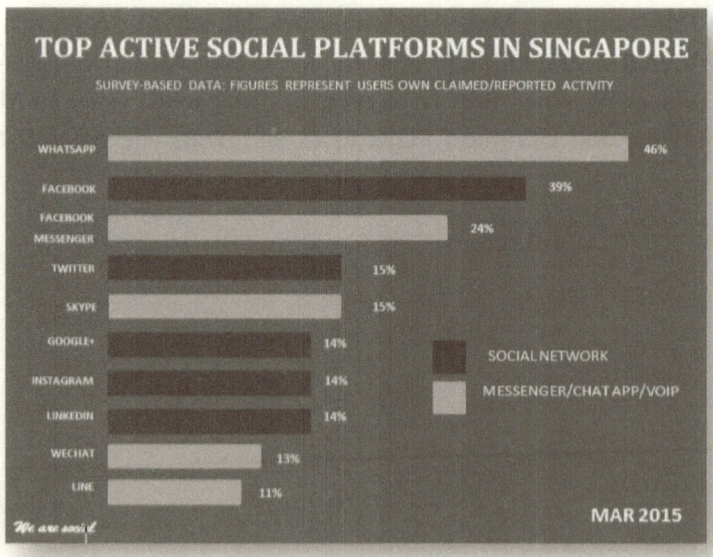

A multicultural society where east meets west, Singapore is a diverse melting pot of cultures and races. With a unique identity that honors tradition yet embraces change, it serves as a regional hub for many international brands. Always at the forefront of technological and economic advances, Singapore is closely aligned with the latest global and regional culture, trends, and news.

The rise of social media globally has deeply influenced and reshaped the way people in Singapore work, collaborate, and consume information—especially within marketing and communications. With the highest global ranking for smartphone penetration and a large population of multi-device users, Singapore's social media landscape is evolving at a fast pace. The island is now home to thriving online communities and sophisticated users for whom social media has become an essential part of everyday life.

While social media giant Facebook remains one of the most used platforms in Singapore, with around 2.4 million daily users, it has become an increasingly competitive and saturated marketplace for brands to connect with fans. As a result, we see more diversification in social media outreach on platforms such as Instagram and other mobile messaging apps.

With WhatsApp as the most popular social network in Singapore, the line between social media and mobile messaging has become increasingly blurred. Users are flocking to other mobile messaging apps as well, such as LINE and WeChat, to connect and engage with their friends, as well as their favorite brands. For example, brands such as Gong Cha, McDonald's, and even Wall Street Journal are already establishing brand channels on LINE as a means to connect with the growing mobile audience.

If this trend continues in 2016, we can expect more convergence between social media and mobile messaging services. More brands will be joining these mobile messaging platforms as they look for ways to connect with customers beyond the social media universe of Facebook and Twitter.

In many ways, Singaporeans use social media like Americans and Europeans. In others, their social habits are unmistakably Asian. The state of social is like so many things in Singapore: a unique combination of East and West, tech-savvy and traditional, energetic yet somewhat restrained.

Facebook is very popular, but when it comes to professional engagement and building a business network, LinkedIn is by far the most popular platform. Having lived and worked in Singapore for many years, I cannot think of anyone over the age of 18, or even younger who does not have a LinkedIn page.

S. Korea

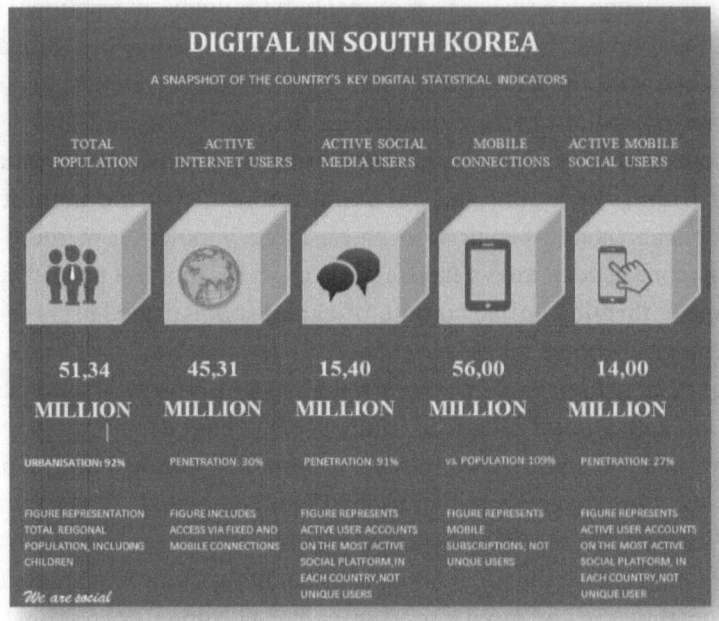

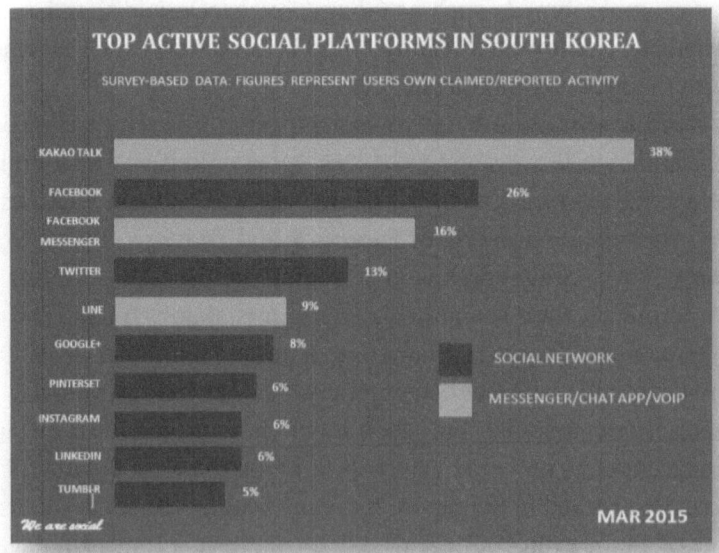

The S. Korean social media market is small compared to some of the other regional markets. But the country makes up the volume gap with the quality of connectivity and data access. South Korea is a world leader in Internet connectivity, as it boasts one of the fastest average connection speeds. To put this into perspective, the download speed in Seoul is 47 Mbps – five times faster than the average cable modem in the United States. S. Korea is also a leader in smartphone use with 78% market share. All this great infrastructure lends itself to the country having the highest digital video viewer penetration in the world, with over 95% of the internet users watching videos online at least once a week over 70% of the S. Koreans in their 20's are active social media users but, for the most part, their focus is, as often is the case with this age group, on fashion, food, shopping and lifestyle.

As for the social media channels go, KakaoTalk has become the number one social network in South Korea, and today boasts approximately <u>48 million</u> monthly active users (MAU). The multi-faceted messaging platform allows free calls, multimedia messaging, event scheduling, and in-app gift shopping. Deloitte named KakaoTalk the number one tech company in the Asia-Pacific region in its recent Technology Fast 500 Asia Pacific survey, which ranks companies based on revenue.

In 2011, Kakao rolled out its advertising platform "Plus Friend" in order to connect users with their favorite brands, celebrities, and media companies.

Line

Messaging platform <u>Line</u> is a subsidiary of South Korea's Naver Corp., and while it has 14 million users in its home country, it has proven most popular in other parts of Asia, especially Japan, Taiwan, Thailand, and Indonesia. Line's annual report for 2014 puts global MAUs at 181 million – with Japan, Taiwan, and Thailand accounting for 92 million.

When it comes to social selling in Korea, the global big players such as LinkedIn are not very popular. Culturally there are some shared traits between Japan and S. Korea, with users not being as comfortable self-bragging and sharing a lot of information about themselves online for business. Most people who know LinkedIn consider it to be a recruiting and job search tool. To succeed in the market one needs to leverage the local big players such as Kakao and Line as much as possible.

Thailand

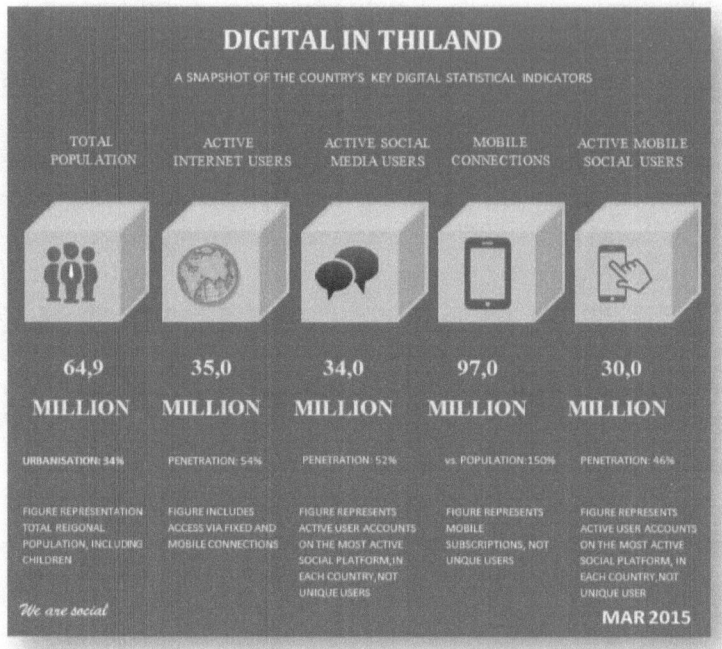

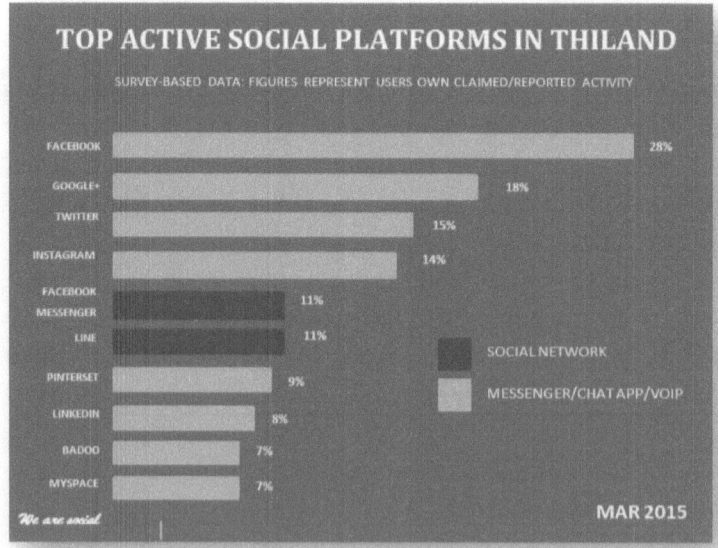

As in other emerging markets, Thailand's social media scene is moving fast and expanding by solid double digits. As in other similar markets, a lot of this growth is coming from the mobile phone market penetration. Thailand closely follows the social media platform trends seen globally, with Facebook, Google+ and Instagram among the most popular social networks. Other regional messaging networks, like WeChat and Line, continue to have strong presence in the region as well.

Due to it's largely rural population (66%), Internet penetration in Thailand remains low at 26%. Interestingly, though, scarce internet access is counterbalanced by an impressive 125% mobile penetration rate, with half of mobile users using social media apps. Although Thais mainly use desktops or laptops for internet access, as internet penetration continues to climb, targeting mobile users will be the key to tapping the Thai market.

Unsurprisingly, Facebook is the biggest social network in Thailand, with 26% of the population using it. However, in the last two years the use of other social apps such as Instagram have exploded. In both 2012 and 2013, Bangkok was home to two of the most Instagrammed locations in the world and remains the 2nd most popular city on Instagram. Thailand has become a destination for Instagram photographers, in part as a result of an increase in smartphones in Thailand's urban centers, but also as a result of urban culture.

When it comes to social selling and B2B engagement, Thailand is still a traditional society with face to face meetings a more common way to engage. Having said that, LinkedIn has a presence there, and you will find a lot of outward looking executives and high-level managers that are active on LinkedIn.

Chapter 13

Tools of the trade

Soon after you sign up for two or more social media accounts, you realize your next challenge is to manage these channels effectively and make sure you don't lose track of your new and expanding relationships online. With all these new social media channels, we are seeing hundreds of new tools to help you better manage your social media engagements. These add-on tools offer you a host of added functionality and automation that most of the social platforms don't offer on their own. Here are some of the key areas that these tools can help:

- Allow you to manage multiple social channels through a single interface and application, so that you can view, post, and share from a single place to multiple channels such as LinkedIn, Facebook, Twitter, Google+, etc.
- Give you a more comprehensive view of a potential client by aggregating the person's various profiles across multiple channels and giving a 360-degree view of the person.
- Help you identify, target, and engage more relevant people in your target market by identifying thought leaders, the shakers and movers.
- Automate the routine tasks such as postings and notifications.
- Track and report on your content effectiveness and engagement by measuring viewing and sharing of your content.
- Manage your time and appointments and integrate them with your calendar to make sure you don't lose opportunities.

Which tools are right for you?

The answer to this question is heavily dependent on what you are trying to achieve. As I mentioned earlier, there are literally hundreds of tools out there, and we are getting dozens more on a weekly basis, each with unique capabilities, target markets, and sometimes target industries. So finding the right apps are not so easy, and you could spend a lot of time and money trying to find one that works well for you. The great thing about having so many choices is that almost all of these social media add-on tools offer you either a basic free version to try out or allow you to test them for free for a while.

Let's now take a look at some of the more popular tools out there that will help you better manage your social media activities and maximize return on your investment. Some of the tools are the ones I have used in the past or use now. Other ones have been around for a while and have a leading position in their patch.

To make it easier remembering which tools do what, I have separated them into three categories by their primary function:

1- **Social media management systems**: more function-rich and often a more comprehensive platform to manage your social media strategy with multiple layers of functionality and security to allow for more scalability.

2- **Social media utilities**: offering add-on functions that could make social media activities easier, faster, and more scalable such as automating content generation and posting.

3- **Social media data analytics**: providing data on the activity level, interaction level with the target audience, and effectiveness of social media efforts.

By all means, this division is not totally black and white as some tools cross over into more than one category. For example, one of my favorite tools, Bitly, helps you have a much shorter URL alias so that it is Twitter-friendly, but also gives you great insight into how many people clicked through your Bitly alias.

Social Media Management Systems: This category includes well-known apps such as Hootsuite, AguraPulse, TweetDesk, SocialEngage, or SproutSocial. They help you keep track and manage your many social network channels. They can enable you to monitor what people are saying about your brand and help you respond instantly. You can view streams from multiple networks such as Facebook, Twitter, and Google+ and post updates or reply directly. With so many networks for businesses to manage, it's no doubt social media management tools have become so popular and relied upon by many companies today.

I personally have used Hootsuite, the basic version which they offer for free for personal use. I found it quite powerful in helping me manage my multiple social channels. If you manage the updates for your business's social networks, it's highly likely that you will have heard of Hootsuite. In a survey from monitoring tool Pingdom, Hootsuite came up as the top social media management system, with over 20% of companies using it to manage their social media empires. TweetDeck was second and SocialEngage third.

Here are the top five reasons I recommend Hootsuite for companies looking at a social media management systems:

1)   Monitor multiple streams in one place.

Probably one of the most compelling reasons to use Hootsuite is the fact that it allows you to manage so many different social networks. It currently allows you to manage:

> Twitter
> Facebook profiles and pages
> LinkedIn profiles and pages
> Google+ pages (not personal profiles)
> Foursquare
> Instagram
> WordPress blogs
> Vimeo, Tumblr, Evernote, Flickr, MailChimp, SlideShare,
> Storify (via third-party apps)
> Many more!

2) Allow a team to manage your social media activities.

If you have more than one person managing your business's social networks, you may encounter challenges around security, division of work, avoiding gaps in services, and basically effective collaboration. Hootsuite allows you to delegate tasks to different people or teams.

3) Managing customer service on Twitter.

Some companies opt to use Twitter as a primary vehicle to handle customer services. If you fall into that category then Hootsuite is probably your best choice. Many utilities and mobile network companies who use Twitter for customer service use Hootsuite because it allows them to delegate customer cases to multiple teams and manage them by the admins.

4) It works across multiple platforms.

This is one advantage in making Hootsuite a web app -- it's easy to make it work on Mac OSX, Windows, Linux, and mobile platforms. Hootsuite indeed works on all modern browsers, and it has a plethora of dedicated mobile apps to help you on the move.

5) Get weekly reports via email.

If you solely or mainly use Hootsuite to manage your social networks, then you will find the weekly analytics report very useful. Each week, Hootsuite sends you an email with a PDF attachment of your click summaries. Hootsuite gives you graphs showing:

> Number of clicks per day
> Geographical information on the people clicking through
> Top referrers
> Most popular links

The good news is that this is free for all users and can be useful to give you a brief overview as to how you are doing on a weekly basis.

Social media utilities: There are an amazing number of tools in this category with very different levels of functionality and sophistication. I personally am a bit too old-fashioned and don't think that more is necessarily better. So I try to be careful about which tools in this category I use because I could get myself too confused and tangled up trying to integrate and leverage too many moving parts. I have listed below some of the more powerful and popular ones. Again, there are too many great tools out there that I could be updating this list almost daily and never finish. With that said, let's look at some of these social media utilities.

Nimble: This tool helps you nurture your relationships and improve your chance of getting a sale. This is a social relationship management tool that helps you identify and engage key influencers, advocates, and customers among your big network of connections. Nimble automatically finds the profiles of your contacts in various social platforms, allowing you to listen and engage with them across different channels.

Nimble also works as your contact manager and engages with your connections through the tool. You are also able to manage your activities, synch up your calendar with Google, create appointments directly in Nimble, build and assign tasks to team members.

As a sales automation tool, Nimble allows you to track opportunities that are generated through the lead management function. Nimble also integrates with a large number of other apps so that you can leverage functionalities in other social media tools including Hootsuite.

One of the functions I really like about Nimble is allowing you to have a single social inbox. Instead of having multiple inboxes in different platforms, you could have them all go into a single inbox, making the task of responding to emails and following up much easier.

Virally App: You know when you want to share some content with a prospect, but you want to make sure at least you get his/her email address for follow-up? Well, the Virally application allows you to restrict access to content until your prospect connects to his/her social network of choice. With Virally you set up a page that asks the user to click and connect to LinkedIn, Facebook, or Twitter. When they do, they get access to your content. The great advantage for you is that now you know a lot more about that person than simply their email address.

This tool could bring you a wealth of information that you didn't have before and could increase your chance of success by allowing you to study up on the prospect before your next contact.

Online appointment tools: I often see a lot of salespeople sending and resending calendar invites, calling prospects and clients back and forth to nail down a meeting time. This task becomes so much harder when the salesperson has to coordinate with more than one person at the client site. A powerful tool to reduce dealing with this tedious and time-wasting task is to have an online appointment scheduler that you can invite your prospects to and ask them to pick a suitable time and schedule the meeting based on your availability. There are a lot of great tools out there with a wide range of services, making it is impossible trying to list them all. Some of the more popular ones I have seen are Appointy, SimplyBook.me, or MyTime.

Make sure to visit our Resources page on our website to learn more about this and other topics that will help you be more successful. www.winningwithsocialselling.com/resources

Social media data analytics: In early chapters we talked a lot about first setting up your social media strategy, goal setting, implementation and review, among other things. But oftentimes an important piece, the metrics, gets overlooked. Here I am going to talk about some of the tools you can use to help you measure the impact of your social media activities and be able to identify which ones are working and which ones are not. For example, wouldn't you want to know which one of your tweets was more popular with your client base? Which ones got retweeted more? Or which one of your blog postings was more popular in a particular country or region?

Here I am going to cover six tools that can help you be more successful in selling by offering you better visibility and insight.

SemRush: You probably haven't heard of this company before. This is a very powerful tool that will tell you the ranking for your site. For example, you can type the URL for the article you had posted to see how it ranks in Google's search result. It shows you what you rank for and what your competitors rank for. It also can help you figure out which Google AdWords you may consider buying.

Woopra: This is a web analytics tool that gives you real-time data about how visitors are interacting with your site. While the visitor is moving through the site, it shows where she went, what actions she took, and where she went after leaving. Woopra has a free version with limited functionality. However, you get a lot more functionality with one of the various paid packages.

Klout: This is one of the first of social ranking measurements that I came across. It offers a daily summary of your company and your team members' social media influence across the top three platforms: LinkedIn, Facebook, and Twitter.

Facebook insights: Facebook's improved Insights service provides you with lots of data on a daily and monthly basis about your active users. Insights service provides information such as daily new likes; daily interactions such as comments; where your visitors came from by country, city, and language; external referrals; and more.

Bitly: This is an interesting tool. This is a great URL shortener that also offers analytics and click data to every link shortened. The click data lets know how effective your social media campaigns are.

Google Analytics: This is a great source of insight on your site traffic and marketing effectiveness. — for free. Create better-targeted ads, track sales and conversions, measure your site engagement goals, track Web-enabled phones and mobile apps, integrate business info, and develop applications that access Google Analytics data. You can also add Google Analytics to your Facebook page.

THE END

Other book by Mark

In "The Winning Formula you will learn:

- Why it is so hard to be good at prospecting and how to overcome the typical pitfalls in becoming more successful.
- What are the fundamental problems with majority of the cold reach techniques
- Who are the right executives that you should be engaging and why
- The most effective techniques in becoming a pipeline generating machine.
- How to leverage the social media in your prospecting efforts
- How to manage gatekeepers